D0982678

# THE LIGHT WITHIN

## A Woman's Book of Solace

JONI WOELFEL

*The Light Within*
*A Woman's Book of Solace*
by Joni Woelfel

Edited by Kass Dotterweich
Cover design by Tom A. Wright
Typesetting by Desktop Edit Shop, Inc.

Published by:      ACTA Publications
                   Assisting Christians To Act
                   4848 N. Clark Street
                   Chicago, IL 60640-4711
                   773-271-1030

Library of Congress Card Number: 00-111391

ISBN: 0-87946-221-3

Printed in the United States of America

Year: 05 04 03 02 01/Printing: 7 6 5 4 3 2 1

# Contents

This book is lovingly dedicated to Melanie Schei and to the many women who supported me and the writing of this book as soul-sisters, mentors, friends and editors.

# Introduction

There is a flow, passion and artistry to Christian feminine spirituality that seeps into such words as womb, blood, maiden passages, life's cycles and ancient mysteries. This very language of birth, rebirth and mystery—the circling and spiraling of our years as we age and journey ever closer to the home country of our souls—is a light within.

Countless women have made that journey home by roads they never imagined they would travel. I, too, have made that journey, often wondering, "How can I survive these sorrows? Where is the light and where are the voices? What do other women have to say? How have other women walked through their pain?" Along this journey, I began connecting with the thoughts, feelings and experiences of close friends, acquaintances, mentors and family—and I assembled a great gathering of voices that helped me chart my own way with greater care and insight. I also found myself hearing the voices of deceased women I had loved and admired, women who remained a part of me much more than I realized. Many of my own forgotten voices also found expression as memories surfaced from that inner sanctum where my deepest thoughts are sheltered.

Descending to this place was a sacred undertaking. As a writer, I felt as if I were venturing into vast chambers of the heart, where I was allowed to serve as a lantern while the stories that chose to reveal themselves became the flame. It was a humbling and profoundly instructive experience.

When women tell the truth about their lives, there is a power that rises in the telling, for themselves and their listeners.

First, there is the passion to share the story authentically, to express the hurt when one is ready, and to get it out in ways that feel safe. Accompanying this passion is the desire to grow from and through the experience. Finally, women need to find meaning and be connected to something that matters—something larger and more embracing than themselves. While their individual spiritual journeys are unique, the lights they carry within pierce the darkness with powerful, universal themes that emerge and overlap. May the reflections shared here bring inner illumination and warmth to the hardships all women face, serving as flames of hope, promise and solace during times of despair, loss and darkness.

# A Lantern in Her Breast

*Then God said, "Let there be light"; and there was light.*

Genesis 1:3

O ne of life's greatest gifts to women can be other women. Through our innate intuition, we have the ability to read between the lines, to know what to say and what not to say. As one woman recently said, "My friends help me renew my enchantment in life and are there to cry with me…when we're not laughing wildly about some irreverent comment."

The gift of feminine relationships with mothers, grand-mothers, sisters, aunts, cousins and women friends enables us to unravel our thoughts to find treasure troves of insight that we didn't know were hidden within. When we speak the words and pour out our uncensored thoughts, then inner worlds to ideas, solutions and faith possibilities begin to open—worlds we never would have found on our own. We women care for each other and are able to reach out and offer solace to other women when it is needed.

Several years ago, certain situations that I had been struggling with nearly got the best of me. It was a dark, disconnected time when I felt like the pilot light in my soul had gone out. During that time, my women friends were steady lanterns of support that helped me find my way back to courage and strength. As I looked back at the amazing inner resurrection I made during that time, I wrote a celebration fable for these women friends:

On the edge of a faraway mountain village, in an old and creaking cottage nestled in a hollow bordered by a forest, there lived a wise woman of undeterminable age. A well-worn footpath led to a small, spring-fed stream below the cottage, just past a clearing that housed a chicken coop, a ramshackle stable and a small pigsty.

The wise woman hummed to herself as she prepared for the party that evening; her friends were coming to celebrate Nothing At All—their favorite celebration. The occasion came about, as you would expect, out of nothing at all. One simply would say to another, "Time to gather?" and sure enough, they would soon be on their way to the cottage in the hollow. For this particular celebration, the wise woman set out her fine china tea cups and an arrangement of dried Indian corn, pumpkins and squash. A loaf of herbal bread rose on the iron cookstove in the corner. It was an unusually cool autumn, hinting at a harsh winter to come.

As night began to fall, the wise woman heard the sound of her friends' laughter echoing in the valley below. Snatching a lantern and shrugging into her old, woolen cloak, she rushed out to greet her guests making their way up the path. As the wind spiraled around the lantern and the flame began to flicker and falter, the woman pressed the lantern ever closer to her breast. It must not be extinguished; it must remain strong and visible.

From a distance, the woman's friends did, indeed, see the light. "Look!" one of them said with wonder. "Our host has a lantern in her breast!" And another sagely replied, "Of course she does, don't we all? Light within never goes out."

*God of Lanterns within Our Breasts, protect the flame when the winds of darkness and trouble swirl around us along our path. Yours is the warmth and light that connects the disconnected, illuminates the past, present and future, and comforts us when the Kingdom of Night falls upon us. Our very bodies are housed within the lantern of your love—within, without, above and below.*

# The Hope of a Baby

*"All this is but the beginning of the birthpangs."*

Matthew 24:8

When a friend was going through a personal crisis, she began to dream about a baby girl. "I must have had those dreams a dozen times," she said. "In the dreams she was my baby and I loved her. But I kept forgetting where I put her and I'd forget to feed her. Then, I would suddenly remember the baby and frantically run around crying, 'Where is my baby? I have to feed her.' She was a good, gentle baby who whimpered only slightly, but when I held her, she felt skeletal and cold. She wasn't warm and weighty the way hearty babies feel when you hold them."

As my friend worked through the problems she was facing, she discovered the mysterious possibility of reinventing herself: "The me I used to be felt like someone trying to put a glove on the wrong hand; it just didn't fit. Those were upheaval times during which my life changed in many ways. Whenever I had one of those baby dreams, I would wake up feeling deeply sad and horrified that I could neglect the baby who needed me so much. Then, as I thought of all I was going through, I realized that the baby was me. She represented how spiritually vulnerable and cold I felt; how emotionally lost and out of touch

I was with myself."

Many women have baby dreams when they are going through an inner birthing process. The baby represents the call of hope and new life. When my friend dreamed of misplacing and forgetting to feed the baby, she was being reminded to nourish and nurture her precious inner self and faith. During this time, she greatly simplified her life and wrapped herself in the swaddling blankets of things and friends that comforted her. Thus held, she was able to descend into the heart and depth of her struggles: "It was as if my spirituality entered a womb, a place of darkness where it could be sheltered and protected while I grew into my own unique self."

Looking back on that time, my friend says that she can see how spiritually starved she was. She had been trying to fit her spirit into a mold, a collective ideal, that wasn't working because it wasn't her. It took several years of birthing pains, but my friend eventually got the message: "In the spirituality of true womanhood, the first thing to go is the mold. After that comes an awakening and a strength that nourish the soul no matter what you go through…because you have found yourself and God's expression in you. You know what you know, and no one can take that away from you." The baby—at last found, fed and cared for—flourishes.

*God Who Mothers Starving Souls, there is a secret nesting place within women that cries out for truth, wholeness and the fullness of what it means to be uniquely woman and spiritual. Thank you for the respect, dignity and appreciation you have for the spirit of every woman, for bringing us the freedom to be ourselves.*

# The Road Home

*They are seeking a homeland.*

Hebrews 11:14

I dreamed about my mother a week before the tenth anniversary of her death. The setting of the dream was a summer workday on the farm where we lived when I was growing up. The afternoon sun drizzled a pleasant warmth on my back that I could feel through the bleached, cotton fabric of my shirt. Overhead, the sky was a vivid blue; and underfoot, the dry, crumbly earth heaved a fertile sigh from between the neatly cultivated rows of beans. The brush of the soybean plants against my hands as I searched for cockle burrs was soft and velvet-like.

As I went about my work, I looked up to see my mother at a distance, coming my way and calling, "It's time to come home." A great feeling of happiness flooded through me as I stood up and watched my mother coming toward me. She was wearing a full plaid skirt, gathered slimly at the waist, a coordinating knit top, black-and-white saddle shoes, and ankle socks. She had on her old black glasses, the ones with the rhinestones. My aunt walked with my mom, linked arm in arm, and the two were laughing together as they moved across the field in my direction.

The dream had such sharp definition that I could see fine smudges of the dry, dusty dirt clinging to Mom's blouse. It was a good thing, the dirt, a healthy thing that added to rather than detracted from the beauty of the dream image.

At the time of this dream, I was worried about a problem, and I did not appreciate the full impact of the dream until much later, when I realized how disconnected I was from myself as a result of fear. The serenity of the dream reminded me to lighten up, to gather in, to "come home" to myself, to God and to the world around me.

But how do we arrive at this homeland in ourselves? How do we come home, or go home to ourselves? One woman makes a list of her fears so she can address them and move on. Her personal fear list reflects many of the common fears women have:

Fear of the unknown;
Fear of not being understood;
Fear of feeling alone or not having friends;
Fear of not meeting the expectations of others or ourselves;
Fear of displeasing others or not fitting in;
Fear of not knowing which struggles to accept and which to fight;
Fear of failing and making mistakes;
Fear of growing old and dying;
Fear of not being smart, slim or pretty enough;
Fear of not being in control;
Fear of becoming stuck and staying there;

Fear of not being a good caretaker;

Fear of being selfish;

Fear of expressing certain feelings, especially anger;

Fear of not being special or respected;

Fear of loss, diminishment or change.

This woman believes that the road home to ourselves is not a road or path at all, but rather a curve of confidence that arcs straight to our heart's center—if, and only if, we are true to ourselves and true to God's voice within us. "Trust these two things," she said, "and you will always find the way."

*God of Winding Roads and Unshakable Women, fear is the dust under our feet that settles by the roadside as we come home to our own heart.*

# The Great Paradox

*You hem me in, behind and before....*
*I am fearfully and wonderfully made....*
*I come to the end—I am still with you.*
Psalm 139:5,14,18

**P**salm 139 is often entitled "The Prayer of a Believing Heart." Throughout the psalm, there is an intricate pattern of contrasting images, assuring us that God is always with us: sitting down and rising up; ascending to heaven and descending to the nether world; on the wings of the dawn and in the night as bright as the day. Those who travel full circle in life know that life consists of the contrast between shadow and light, faith and doubt, suffering and comfort. One woman calls her hardship experience the Great Paradox:

> It's a journey and story of contrasts, a letting go of superficiality and a clinging to the truths of the heart, letting "religion" fade so that true spirituality can take root. In hardship, I have found nearly every belief and prayer tested; not just once, but over and over. I have also found that revelation comes by active participation in the process. I have experienced loss in many ways, but there has always been a gain in the loss. When I am at my most vulnerable, I must also be tough-skinned, willing to keep on, which is again the

paradox of hardship. It is from all these foundations that the transforming and transcending process springs, like a shoot of green grass that, despite all odds, pushes itself up through the smallest of cracks in the blacktop surface.

When I think of enduring my own adversities, I think of the classic children's story, *The Velveteen Rabbit*. Through love, and after much wear and tear, the rabbit becomes "real." This and the ability to endure come to him little by little, just as the wise skin horse (the epitome of ancient wisdom) promised. The tattered horse, himself, had endured the "becoming real" process until he was reduced to nothing but soft skin—because a tough-skinned demeanor blocks out love, yet love is the only thing that makes us strong. Only love has the power to transform our hardships into bearable, even promising opportunities. If the skin horse has a message, I think it would be, "Press on…for your own sake and for the sake of others who will need your wisdom and hope."

*Great Physician of Tattered Horses and People in Need of Mending, becoming fearfully and wonderfully real is the greatest thing that ever happens to us. Help us to never underestimate the power and consolation of this gift. When we are hemmed in, let it be with love.*

# Bend or Break

*The human spirit will endure sickness;*
*but a broken spirit—who can bear?*
Proverbs 18:14

The wind is blasting through our village, knocking things over and rattling the windows of our old house. My outdoor, plastic love seat is lying upside down in the flower bed—right where the wind hurled it. The wind is so fierce, in fact, that it knocked the stem off my pumpkin, which irks me. I look up at the trees, which are taking a direct hit from the wind as well, and I am amazed at the deluge of yellow leaves as they are yanked from their moorings and dashed to the ground, there to be blown about even more. I notice, too, that my one lone cornstalk (of which I am very proud ) also does battle with the wind. I guess I could run out and tie it securely to the deck so it can't blow around, but if I do that the wind will simply snap it off at the top. In order to save it, I have to let it bend with the wind, hoping that it will be supple enough to withstand the onslaught.

It does not take much imagination to parallel these thoughts to the fury experienced by those enduring hardship. I look at the love seat, the pumpkin stem and the leaves, and I know their sense of being uprooted from where they belong. I look, too, at the cornstalk, still in the midst of battle, and I want to say, "Hang in there; you either bend with it or you break, but there is a vast space between those two little words."

For many of us, there would not be enough ink to list all the times we need to bend lest we break. To bend spiritually is an attitude, a resilience of the soul, knowing that there are things we have to do whether we like them or not. We all have to get out of bed on cold, dark mornings. We all have to work. We all have to carry on and get back up when heartache makes us feel cut off at the knees or ripped from what we took for granted. Relationships change; finances plummet; jobs are lost; parents, spouses and children die prematurely; health deteriorates; promises get broken. Troubles of every kind can and often do occur when we least expect them—and to bend will be our only chance of surviving.

*God of Broken Souls, when suffering ties us down and life brings a pounding onslaught of pain and challenge, help our spirits to relax and "go supple" so we will not break. It's when we go rigid with fear, sorrow and despair that we lose hope. Especially then, help us to hear your whispered love: "Try bending...you can do it. It will help, I promise. Bend into Me."*

# The Evolution of Polly Pure-Heart

*"Blessed are the pure in heart, for they will see God."*

Matthew 5:8

**P**olly Pure-Heart sees the world through rose-tinted glasses. She thinks there is no problem or wrong that cannot be fixed or overcome. The walls in her house are painted bright yellow; she has artificial silk roses on her table that always bloom; she volunteers for nearly every needy cause that comes her way; her children excel; her husband loves to help with the dishes; and her dog never has fleas. Polly Pure-Heart wakes up singing each morning, believing that her life is perfect.

Some say Polly Pure-Heart is like a butterfly before it moves out of its cocoon; she is a woman who has not yet come into her own. My sister, however, pointed out to me that many women want to be Polly Pure-Heart and that this doesn't necessarily mean that they have no inner depth. She says women deepen and change in their own time, shaped by their unique life experiences and responses. As a teacher suggested, "A woman should not be considered naive just because she hasn't known as much trouble as another."

One woman, who had experienced a lot of hardship in her life, wrote:

I lost my sense of innocence early in life. I always thought I would have an all-American life. Instead, my parents died when I was young, I became disabled from a disease, and I was divorced at an early age. Finally, I asked, "What have I ever done to deserve all this? I've tried to be a good girl all my life." Sometimes I told God that I needed to start my life over because I didn't turn out right. My edges were all burnt and broken off, and I felt sure my life wasn't supposed to turn out this way. I likened myself to being baked in the oven too long, like a gingerbread-woman cookie. All I ever wanted was a simple, happy life, as in a fictional Polly Pure-Heart melodrama. When that didn't happen, I realistically found what I had been seeking all along: a pure spirit that aspired to an authentic spiritual relationship with God, the earth, others and myself.

Another woman wrote:

I've never been one to ask for help, but major surgery made me feel so useless at first. For a time, I felt completely alone in my recovery, overwhelmed and limited. I had no motivation and was utterly exhausted, but sleep wouldn't come. I kept telling myself that these bad days were only good days in disguise, but my heart did not feel it. On top of everything else, my doctor told me I was premenopausal, which was probably why I felt too old to be young and too young to be old. I was filled with self-pity which, to me, was bad. Then one day a friend asked me, "Why do you think it's okay to feel empathy for others but not yourself?" She described self-pity as a valid emotion in which the soul is simply expressing the need for comfort. Eventually, I bought myself a set of watercolors and a canvas and began to paint. I was astonished at the pure beauty and sense of satisfaction that unfolded through my own brush strokes and pain—my own creation!

Although I've told and retold the story of Pure-Heart many times, she continues to elude me. Just when I think I have her figured out, another layer develops and I have to go back to the drawing board. She keeps transforming, refining and unfolding as aging, joy, life and trial bring gifts of personal evolution. I keep returning to how her story ends, confident that someday I can say, "Polly Pure-Heart becomes a wise sage who reveres life, believing that each new day holds comfort and goodness waiting to happen. Her name, representing the ancient, eternal voice of hope, light and spring, lives on forever in the hearts of all women who believe."

*Hovering, Ever-Present Mother God, you encircle your arms around purity in us like a beloved child that you are raising.*

# Teach the Children Young

*But there is forgiveness with you.*

Psalm 130:4

S ometimes we women make mistakes that devastate us. Remorse fills us so deeply that we feel we can never forgive ourselves. One woman told of an experience that happened over thirty-five years ago, when she was ten years old. The mistake she made was so shattering to her at the time that she never told her mom, dad or friends. She wrote:

> I was always a tomboy as a kid. I love animals and had created what I called a pet hospital in a shed. In the pet hospital, I had a large, screened-off enclosure filled with straw for my beloved pet rabbit named Spicey. She was the color of ginger, with a tiny, white diamond on her forehead and white paws.
>
> One day I noticed that there was movement under the deep straw of her pen. I decided that a mouse or two had perhaps moved into the old shed, so I planned to clean out the pen and put in new straw. Since Spicey was so tame, I just locked her out of her pen and left her free to roam the lawn, garden and woods. She always stayed close by. I noticed that she kept going back to her old pen and pawing at the

screen like she wanted to get back in. I repeatedly said, "Spicey, you don't want to go back into that smelly old pen until I clean it." Then, I would carry her back outside again, but she still kept trying to get back in, which I ignored.

A week later, I finally got around to cleaning out the pen. I took a shovel and rake and began pushing back the straw. Small tufts of fur came loose with the straw. Puzzled, I knelt down for a closer look. In a corner, as I pulled the straw back, I saw a soft, downy nest that Spicey had made from her own fur. In the nest were six baby rabbits, all dead. Dry-eyed, I cradled their cold bodies in my hands, anguish searing my broken heart unlike anything I had ever experienced. Their death was my fault; they had starved to death and I felt like a murderer. I wanted to cry, "I didn't know! I didn't know!" but I was too numb with the shock of what had happened.

Gathering the small bodies with Spicey following close behind, I took them into the deep woods and buried them in the rich, black soil, marking each grave with a small stick. I was only ten, an innocent child. As I knelt there alone on my knees, I'd never felt more forlorn or hopeless. The woods seemed silent with grief, while an old chicken hawk circled around a twisted cedar tree in the distance. I never cried, and I was not myself for the rest of the summer.

Gradually, the resilience of youth and wonder helped me move on, but I never consciously forgave myself. I didn't know how, so I just forgot. But forgetting is not the same as healing. Forgetting is not life-giving; it's just burying and postponing.

As an adult many years later, something happened in my life that triggered that long-ago memory. Prayerfully, I went back to myself in my imagination. I envisioned the adult me taking the hand of the child me. I imagined saying, "You are not alone in this horror. I will comfort you and guide you through this. We will bury the baby rabbits together. Say you are sorry to Spicey and give the babies back to the earth and to God—and weep." I imagined the child me releasing the tears of guilt and sorrow. Then, the adult me instructed the child me, "Now say the words aloud, *I forgive myself.*" As my child self said those words, I imagined wiping away her tears, embracing her and saying, "Now, let your heart heal."

*God Who Loves Children, Animals and All That Is Vulnerable, your hand is there all our lives, guiding us, upholding us and keeping us. The very planet moves to the timeless rhythm of your words, "Let your heart heal."*

# God's Love Is Like a Grandma

*"Is wisdom with the aged,
    and understanding in length of days?"*
                                    Job 12:12

When I am feeling particularly creative, I sometimes wonder what my beloved grandmother would say about life if she were still here. During these times, I pretend that I am my grandmother, and I begin writing as I imagine she would have written. For example, I imagine her in a nursing home and let her voice flow through the chambers of my heart, as if she were writing this story:

> I like to think of this place where I live as my final depot, the place where I rest a spell between passenger trains that will take me to heaven. Most of the people I knew are dead now—and I am not afraid of death. I am proud of the age I have reached and feel like it is an accomplishment. In my sleep, I see my parents and my husband; in my dreams I am not old or confined to this wheelchair. I have become a very matter-of-fact woman.
>
> I had a farm once, where I milked cows and cooked on a black iron cookstove that I filled with corncobs. I made bread every other day, and even now

I can smell the fragrance of it baking and filling my large white farmhouse from top to bottom. Do you know, pheasants were so plentiful in our grove that I once took the shotgun and got two for supper?

I was always a strong, sturdy woman, not physically feeble like I am now. I loved hanging sheets and my husband's overalls on the clothesline. I made handmade soap in the shade behind my house, and I loved to have company. In my era, people visited each other for entertainment. I miss those days and all my friends, the sound of my husband playing his fiddle and talking. When people came, we talked and talked and talked.

I never told anyone this, but I was lonely sometimes. My husband was a good man, but he was quiet by nature. I never made a big deal out of it; people didn't back then, you know. When I wanted to hear a friendly voice, I put on the radio and listened to old-time music and a Jesus preacher that I liked. I listened to the radio a lot. I had a huge garden, chickens, beloved grandchildren and the farm to keep me busy. I was good at being busy and working. These things were all I ever knew, and it was enough. It was better than enough.

My body sits in this wheelchair, but my mind takes me back to the farm every day. Sometimes when I wake up in the morning, I think I am there and that I need to get up and start the coffee and fry bacon and eggs before we do the barn chores. Yesterday I heard an aide say to a nurse—right in front of me—that I was talking out of my head when I said I heard the train whistle calling to me at night in my dreams. I might have been—and I don't mind what they think. They just don't know that when you are old it is easy to live between different worlds—the present and the past. I try to be patient with them. I did say, "Dear, wait until you get old," but the aide just harrumphed and left. The nurse stayed a minute, though, and laughed with me. After that, I took a nap, and in my dreams I went back to the farm again. *I'm old enough to go where I want.*

Pleasantly surprised at this story that emerges from my imagination, I smile. "Thanks, Grandma, that was good advice, coming just when I needed it."

*God Who Transcends Time and Space, the human spirit is ageless, resilient and capable of standing up for itself in a multitude of creative ways.*

# Scrapes, Bumps and Dreams

*I lie down and sleep;*
  *I wake again, for the Lord sustains me.*
  *I am not afraid.*

Psalm 3:5-6

Conflict Training 101 is a course in which we women could all use a refresher from time to time. All of us have people in our lives who have the power to test feelings beyond the normal everyday levels. Sometimes, if we let our guard down and forget who these "risk" people are, no matter how pure our intentions we can get emotionally burned or skinned up when we least expect it.

How can we tell when we're being tested beyond our normal level of endurance? Can we protect ourselves from being emotionally scarred?

When I am under a lot of stress, faced with a challenging situation, my dreams will tell me. In fact, I have two repetitive dreams that remind me that I could be feeling out of control. In the first dream, I am driving a car that only goes backwards, won't steer correctly, and has no brakes. The other dream involves a raging, treacherous river that I am trying to cross. The water is brown, deep and swirling, and has lots of whirlpools that can suck me under if I get too close. These dreams always carry the same messages: First, I am feeling troubled; second, I need to examine what is happening or has recently happened and determine whether it is an old issue that needs more work or a new one altogether; third, I have to ask myself if I need to step back from something (or someone) in my life, make a decision to move forward or postpone any change at all for the time being.

Our dreams reveal to us inner conditions that need our attention. Although at times they may be nothing more than the result of our eating too many pickles before bed, generally they affirm progress, help us work through problems, and vividly portray the deepest longings, hurts, activity and healing that is going on in our psyche.

Dreams have their own language and symbolism, and they don't let us fool ourselves. Many times they invite us to face truths or unfinished business that we don't want to address when we're awake and busy. They also challenge us to view ourselves as students rather than victims when disturbing experiences make us feel threatened. The world of dreams can help keep us in touch with our emotional life. They accurately portray the inner spiritual language of our hardships, helping us to regroup and gather in our hope…or to start over.

*God of Slumber, now I lay me down to sleep; I pray to you my soul to keep.*

# The Princess and the Path

*By paths they have not known*
*I will guide them.*

Isaiah 42:16

When we women must cope with unresolved heartbreak, we ask, "Why am I here at this moment in time, in this particular place? What is the meaning of my life? How can I possibly move on from here? Will God be able to get me through this?" One woman wrote, "I have found that we carry some things inside us that can never be fixed or finished—like not having a chance to say 'Goodbye and I love you' to my daughter who died in an accident." Another young woman, whose father died when she was a baby, said, "I never even got to say hello, and I have needed my dad all my life." Another wrote, "In the heat of an argument, I said crushing things I didn't mean to someone I love dearly, and my remorse nearly kills me when I think of what I said." For all three of these women, there is no going back to the way things were.

"Closure" is a trendy term in self-help books today. We are told that, through image or prayer work, we can create spiritual closure to things that hurt or haunt us. Many years ago, I began writing a fable about a princess who was on a significant journey. The irony is, I never was able to write an ending that seemed right for the story. Today, however, that story remains one of my all time favorite tales *because* it doesn't have an ending or offer any answers. The story goes:

As the starless night fell upon the meadow, releasing a heavy-handed mist of dew, the princess stood at her cottage door, dimly silhouetted by the shrouded blur of the moon. Clammy moisture beaded her upper lip, while her wavy hair crinkled in the humidity. Sighing with resignation, her heart tattered but ready, the princess picked up her small valise, stepped slowly and deliberately down the worn, wooden steps, and walked out into the unknown. In the distance, from deep within the nearby woods, there echoed an eerie howling. Although not an unfamiliar sound, it still caused the hair on the back of the princess's neck to stand up.

As she walked along, the princess watched the woods begin to shimmer—as she knew they would. The magic was beginning. As the trees began to sway, she caught her breath, knowing that the Path would soon open up and she would be required to journey along it as she had many times in the past.

The princess stepped confidently forward, the dripping clover immediately soaking her soft, leather traveling boots. The worst moment of fear and regret had passed, and trust took its place. The princess knew she had to go—and so she did. Experience had taught her not to waste time protesting once the waiting was over.

Within minutes she reached the meadow's edge bordering the woods—and there time seemed to stand still. Gradually, the thick trees silently parted, revealing a faint, luminous path that lay before her...

The princess is an experienced traveler. She is dressed sensibly for the journey; she is familiar with the voice of heartache (represented by the distant howling); she knows that her sorrow is going to take her somewhere into the deep woods of her psyche; she realizes that her faith will be tested. She also knows that trust in something beyond herself will follow on the heels of the worst moment of pain and fear.

I love this ongoing, unfinished story. It reminds me that God prepares a safe path for all of us—a path that unfolds as our hardships unfold. Watching the princess, we get a sense that things will turn out all right, even though what lies ahead isn't revealed. God always provides a path, if not an ending.

*God of Heartaches in Progress, sometimes our only comfort comes from believing that you go before us no matter what happens. When we can't have closure, you yourself are closure to tragic things that can't be fixed.*

# An Empty Nest and Beyond

*Neither death, nor life, nor angels, nor rulers, nor things present, nor things to come, nor powers, nor height, nor depth, nor anything else in all creation, will be able to separate us from the love of God.*

Romans 8:38-39

When our seventeen-year-old son died unexpectedly, my family and I were stunned, our grief inconsolable. One day, a friend sent me a magazine clipping of a pair of hands cradling an empty nest and reaching toward heaven. Above the nest, being drawn toward a sacred realm of light, was an egg. The image evoked a powerful sense of connection for me.

Just weeks prior to our son's death, I had started work on this book. Since I anticipated that my writing would involve a great deal of inner work and personal incubation, I had placed an egg by my computer—a powerful symbol of new life and, for me, a symbol of this new phase of my journey. In many ancient traditions, in fact, the egg represents immortality. At the time, of course, I had no way of knowing what that small egg would come to mean to me. Following our son's death, I often thought about dashing out into the woods and smashing the egg against a tree as an expression of my grief and desperation. Somehow, though, I just couldn't bring myself to do that.

After four months, however, when my egg began to spoil, I finally knew what I had to do. I carefully placed the spoiling egg in a tiny brass pail and headed for the woods, following a familiar trail, to a place where a creek splashes across a rock-strewn stream bed just below a beaver dam. This has always been a sacred prayer place for me, overshadowed by what I call The Great Grandmother Trees.

Standing there, I prayed that God would comfort my family, our son's friends and me in our grief. Speaking at length about the sorrow, the despair, the horror, the wonder of our lives, the mystery and hope of feeling our son was "gone but not truly gone," I clutched to my breast the small pail holding the decaying egg. As I prayed, a giant great horned owl flew silently into view and landed on a large branch of a Great Grandmother Tree, seeming to keep vigil directly above me. I could see his round, wide eyes, which seemed both solemn and benevolent.

As the owl watched, I slipped the egg out of the pail and let it slide into the still water at my feet. Lingering for only a moment, it slowly began to tumble into the middle of the stream, pulled along by the gentle current. I watched, feeling it was important to witness this journey. Then, a surprising thing happened. For no apparent reason, the egg drifted back toward me and came to rest, again, at my feet. It occurred to me in that moment that *letting go brings love back to us*, in different and powerful dimensions we really can't comprehend. With tears stinging my eyes, I watched the egg rest briefly at my feet and then float back again into the middle of the creek, where it resumed its slow journey downstream. As I glanced up, the owl lifted silently, his monstrous wings sweeping him from sight.

Night had begun to fall and I could barely see as I made my way back through the woods. It seemed to me as if God had sent the owl to keep vigil, thereby assuring me that I was doing the right thing in releasing my son, my sorrow, my dreams and hopes, allowing the stream of life and God's care to surround, enfold and carry us all. The egg seemed so small and fragile in the stream, I felt very protective of it—but I sensed that it was time to trust, to symbolically let it go to wherever it was meant to go.

In the near darkness, the naked branches of the winter trees were silhouetted against the sky, and I could see the many empty nests the tree lifted heavenward, as if in supplication, like prayers. Reminded of the magazine clipping that my friend had sent me, I felt somehow comforted. Clutching the now empty brass pail to my breast, as I had earlier, I thought of "emptiness," of an empty cocoon, of Christ's tomb—and then I thought of resurrection. As gratitude for hope filled me, I knew I would find the courage to go on.

*God of Empty Nests and Loved Ones Who Have Crossed Over, there is an invisible realm of spirit that weaves itself into and beyond the world we see with only the human eye. Whether we are in or out of the nest, whether we know it or not, and no matter what happens, we are never without the embrace of your unceasing vigil of love.*

# Staircase to Heaven

*"I am the light of the world. Whoever
follows me will never walk in darkness but
will have the light of life."*

John 8:12

In mythology, climbing a mountain often represents progression toward spiritual enlightenment, and the higher the mountain the closer one is to God. The journey up the mountain can also symbolize struggling with insurmountable challenges, as illustrated by the following two friends.

One of these women keeps a large, cherished painting that she created herself prominently displayed on the wall of her open-stairway landing. The painting, called "Staircase to Heaven," depicts a robe-clad sage at the top of a mountain holding a lantern. The light from his lantern sheds a beacon down the mountainside to a struggling wayfarer and to the distant village beyond.

The woman writes:

I was thinking about how I love rocks, especially perfectly round, smooth rocks, like the ones I collect. It dawned on me that my "Staircase to Heaven" painting is strewn with rocks—but they are not round rocks. Rather, they are pointed and jagged, piled one

39

on top of the other to make a mountain of rocks that portrays the image of a staircase. To me, the man at the top holding the lantern represents God as a father, sending light to me when I am lost and struggling to find my way.

This woman goes on to describe a time in her life when she felt like Anne of Green Gables, when she was in the "depths of despair." During that time, her spirit was so numb that she wouldn't let anyone near it, not even herself. "Something was very wrong," she says, "but at the time, I did not recognize the fact that I was becoming clinically depressed. Part of the trouble was that I didn't know how to rest. Sometimes I felt I would go crazy." At that time in her life, the woman had started to refinish her beautiful wooden stairway:

> I asked myself why I started at the bottom. Just like in my painting, I was like the figure seeking the light— starting at the bottom, looking up, searching. I was striving to be this round, smooth, steadfast rock, while my life seemed full of jagged, pointed rocks that hurt. As time went on and I got better, I realized that the jagged rocks in my life did not rip me apart as I once thought they would. Rather, they had become hand- and foot-holds for me, the steps on my stairway to heaven that taught me many things. Each struggle was connected to the next, creating a certain momentum that carried me closer to God. It was as if God was holding out a lantern of love to me when I felt loveless and forlorn.

The other woman, facing major upheaval in her life as well, also spoke of a mountain. Through image work, she was able to realize the promise of God's warmth and light. She wrote:

> There was a time in my life when my heart felt pierced up through my feet, as if I were standing on a frozen mountain ledge barefoot while a blizzard raged around me. Life was like a white-out snowstorm in which I couldn't see two inches in front of me. I imagined pressing against the mountain cliff, shivering in a thin, flannel nightgown, clutching a scrap of blanket to my chest, hearing only the sound of the wind. I thought of running away, but where would I go?

As this woman was praying, she delved deeper into her mountain snowstorm fantasy, feeling as if the spiritual heat in her body had drained away, all except for a pinpoint in her chest:

> It was as if the world consisted of only me and that dot. I thought of Genesis, when in the beginning the earth was a formless void and darkness covered the face of the deep. The first thing God created was light. Even when I felt as if my own light had gone out, the light of God within me remained eternal, a powerful pinpoint of hope and comfort that did not beckon to me from afar but began melting, thawing, illuminating and warming me from the inside out.

*God of Staircases to Heaven, one minute ray of light from you can move and transform mountains of heartache. You only ask that we believe and look up.*

# Over the Fence

*"Honor your father and your mother."*

Mark 7:10

**O**ne woman's story tells how suffering and heartache actually brought her a gift. Her full awareness of the gift spoke to her from a greeting card she had sent to a friend:

The card showed two children jumping over a fence on which was posted "No Trespassing." In the photo, the children were leaping over the fence as if it were the most natural thing in the world—oblivious to the sign. Looking at the children on that card, I got a sense of some great adventure waiting beyond that fence—an invitation to unexplored places that had been off-limits before. It made me feel that I really wanted to go there and wild horses would not keep me away. That was how I felt as I recovered from a terrible hurt in my life. As I healed, I felt as if I'd crossed a fence, because I saw life so differently. I was no longer intimidated by what I perceived as cultural or faith boundaries that shouldn't be crossed. I wanted to draw my own conclusions rather than simply accept what I was taught by my traditional upbringing.

Because I didn't know where to turn at first, I

traveled alone with no one to guide me, feeling my way in the dark, trusting and knowing I was changing—and there was no stopping it. The only thing I didn't have was the validation and language for what was happening to me. I kept thinking about being on the fringes, out there in no-person's-land, going wild and feeling drawn to feathers, rocks, rivers, trees, and earthy colors, music, fabrics, spices, and books. I felt I was unraveling and, for the first time in my life, examining the beliefs that directed my entire life to that point.

I was so frustrated; I sensed a major piece was missing but I didn't have a name for it. I actually felt a bit rebellious, knowing that my search was drawing me to the study of a theology that would not meet with approval from certain people whose opinion mattered to me. Despite that prick of criticism, though, I began studying the feminine nature of God. It was like coming home to myself, an 'aha' moment that honored and blended beautifully with my love of God as Father.

Following this awakening in my life, I began to find a language that was *my* language. I began listening to my body, my feminine cycles, my intuition, and I began to trust in the synchronicity of events and experiences as the framework of my hardships began to make sense. There was such comfort and wonder in this; I was like a child who had trespassed over a fence into a homeland that was hers to begin with. I had a whole new world to explore.

I learned a powerful lesson in that experience: A personal religion that cannot hold up to scrutiny and questions is no religion at all. It was as if an energizing wind blew through my traditional faith, leaving my previous beliefs not so much diminished as uplifted, renewed and enfolded.

*Sweeping, Swooshing God Who Knows No Boundaries, no one loves balance, freedom and wind more than you do!*

# Light Bearers

*Even the darkness is not dark to you;*
*the night is as bright as the day,*
*for darkness is as light to you.*

Psalm 139:12

S ometimes women's faith in humanity can waver. When we think of the violence and cruelty people are capable of, it can make us feel like withdrawing from the human race— especially when we think of the atrocities done to women and children, the aged and the handicapped. When women think of the women's holocaust of the seventeenth century, when thousands of midwives, herbalists, healers and village-wise women were burned at the stake, we want to cry out, "The past matters! Where were the saviors and champions of the human race? How can insanity like that enter the hearts and minds of a people?"

In this enlightened age, you would think that intelligence, learning from the mistakes of the past, and just plain being civilized would alter the violence the world has always known—yet it continues. When Pope John Paul II called for forgiveness regarding the Holocaust, the Inquisition and the Crusades in one of his millennium messages to the people of the world, many hearts leapt in hope. His message of not only bestowing forgiveness but also *asking* for forgiveness on a global scale, especially regarding patriarchal injustices against women and the violence against indigenous people, deeply touched the hearts of the faithful. His message makes us want to stand up proudly and be counted among those who believe in and follow the Light of the World.

When I wrote this at 4:00 a.m., one lone bird outside my window began to sing—insistently and all by itself—in the darkness, before the blush of dawn announced a new day and awakened the other song birds. That lone note made me think of my friend, Wren. During an especially challenging time for me, Wren would often leave homemade soup on my door step—without any words, without a note. She would arrive quietly, leaving only the soup and her invisible prayers of kindness and support. How did she know my soul desperately needed that soup? I certainly hadn't told her. Yet, bringing soup was Wren's way of singing in the darkness, offering her lone, powerful, enfolding and nurturing voice of strength in her soup and in her prayer.

Have you ever had to sing by yourself in the darkness? Perhaps the message is that many other voices are there—but they've just not awakened in their hearts yet. Remember this when you feel alone, as if no one cares or wants to hear your heart's truth. Remember that truth does not always awaken fully, early or even at all in some people. *You are called to nothing less than simply to know your own song and to release it to a hurting and violent world.*

*God Who Embraces Humankind, the awakening beauty and astonishing light-shedding possibilities of the human soul far surpasses the darkness of the world.*

# A Beast Called Anger

*Put away from you all bitterness and wrath and anger...be kind to one another, tenderhearted, forgiving one another as Christ has forgiven you.*

Ephesians 4:31-32

Forgiveness is a word we women often dance around, using excuses or psychological jargon to explain and defend our shortcomings. We say fashionably, "I wasn't in touch with my inner child" or "I was momentarily disconnected from positive energy." We don't like to say, "I was acting like a jerk. Would you forgive me?"

Years ago, a young mother was so consumed with anger that she poured out her feelings into a short fantasy story:

Startled out of a nightmare-ridden sleep, I rose on an elbow in the dark of my bedroom to listen to distant noises: glass breaking, muffled growling, and the sound of someone rummaging through my refrigerator. Creeping down the stairs with great caution, I suddenly froze in horror on the bottom step. There, beneath my feet, I could feel crumpled cookies and, in the dim light, I could see junk thrown all over the house. Three empty cartons of milk, nine apple cores, and four empty bags of potato chips littered my path to the kitchen. I recognized the disorder and, without a doubt, I knew who the culprit was.

The name of this monster is Anger—and he was no stranger here, even though he had not been allowed to pay us a visit for quite some time. Perhaps his cousin, Irritability, told him there was an opening at our house. No matter; it was apparent that he was planning to make up for lost time, because I could see that he had brought three of his crafty accomplices with him: Self-Pity, Self-Righteousness and Anxiety. They made quite a foursome, and naively we had gone to bed, leaving them free to roam the house and our thoughts.

The worst part about this gruesome visitor, Anger, is that we saw him approaching our door and did nothing to thwart his coming in. In fact, we actually provided him a feast—of negative feelings. Usually, we can clear the feast table and send him on his way, but not this time. Instead, we kept offering him more tidbits and providing him with his favorite kind of entertainment.

Well, I'd had it! I had allowed this bizarre party to go entirely too far. I knew I had to rid our home of these uninvited and definitely unwanted visitors. Through all the hubbub, I suddenly saw with clarity how these four had been cheering us on, adding fuel to the hurts of our home, while my husband and I were caught up in petty arguments—one after the other.

Sensing I was on to them, the intruders suddenly stopped their pranks and stared at me, waiting to see if I would speak the words of banishment. I even sensed their frenzy as they seemed to regroup for a final stand. Ah, but it was too late for them, and they knew it!

I turned around, went back upstairs, awakened my husband, and whispered sincerely, "I'm truly sorry, Dear. Can you forgive me?" As he took me in his arms, I could feel the house around us become absolutely filled with pure, sacred silence. Not a monster remained.

*God of All That Goes Bump in the Night, our friends Self-Control and Reason always stand quietly by the door, awaiting our invitation to enter. We need only say the word.*

# Love Too Small

*Above all, maintain constant love for one another....Like good stewards of the manifold grace of God, serve one another with whatever gift each of you has received.*

1 Peter 4:8,10

O ne of the most challenging paradoxes for spiritual women to understand is that there are truly complicated people in the world. We always want to think that people are essentially good and would never intentionally hurt another human being. The reality is that the behaviors of others do hurt us, sometimes deeply. One woman shares the pain she suffered in her relationship with her stepfather:

> When our gentle father died, our mother could not bear to be alone. She met a man who is what one would call a smooth talker, and soon the two of them got married. But I disliked the man from the moment I laid eyes on him. I felt there was something fishy about him, but my older brother and I kept our opinions to ourselves, hoping things would work out for Mom's sake.
>
> Before long though, things began to fall apart. Among all his other problems, our stepfather could

not hold a job and he began to verbally abuse Mom. Eventually, her personality began to change and she became withdrawn. I could hardly believe that someone like this man had come into the midst of our small, pure-hearted family.

Years later, when Mom died, the man disappeared, and we never saw him again. We did hear that he had died alone, taking with him a bad reputation that followed him his entire life.

With candid honesty, this woman admits that her stepfather taught her something about herself: " I learned how easy it is for me to write people off. I think I wrote him off the day I met him." It took many years for this woman to acknowledge that her stepfather was a child of God—just as she was. With time, she actually recalled a vulnerable side to him: the need to impress people; his small gestures of trying to be kind or to do the right thing. He was, in fact, not without sensitivity, even though it was warped and undeveloped. Why his love was so small and narrow is something she will never understand—and she says she doesn't try.

If he were alive today, this woman says, she still would cross the street to avoid him. "But my heart bleeds a little for him," she insists, "and I am glad for this small grace that comes when I imagine him as who he could have been had his capability to love and shelter been whole."

*God of People Hurt by the Failings of Others, perhaps you have a mending place for those who are scarred by the shortcomings of those who cannot shoulder caretaker responsibilities entrusted to them. Yield great healing from small graces, God; compensate and weave love and wisdom gathered from secret, holy places reserved just for the neglected or abused.*

# A Woman Alone

*I opened to my beloved,*
  *but my beloved had turned and*
  *was gone.*

Song of Solomon 5:6

Even the most caring people sometimes fall into the grip of addiction. A woman whose husband came from a family of hard-drinking men recalls how her husband's addictions actually taught her one of life's most valuable lessons: "I had to learn—the hard way—that another person's problems do not have the power to destroy you, even if that person happens to be a soul mate. I also learned that sometimes we have to stand alone, relying solely on our own strength and God's grace."

The cliché "I'm always the last to know" was true for this woman. She knew that something was terribly wrong; the connection between her and her husband was gone. She wrote:

> But I never suspected that he was drinking at work or that he had started to gamble. Many nights I would sit with the phone in my lap until 3:00 in the morning, crying softly, not knowing where he was or who to call.
>
> Finally, when life crashed around us, I became consumed with questions: How could he do this?

How could he betray and neglect our family? How could he lie?

The counseling began, the antidepressants, the black time of sorting out, forgiving, healing, false starts and relapses. With time, I learned that gambling and alcoholism can be diseases with beast-like claws that sink in and don't let go. I also experienced, firsthand, the reality of the Resurrection, as I watched my husband find his way again and completely recover.

I now know that journeys between soul mates can temporarily separate couples, like a fork in the road where one goes to the right and the other goes to the left—each going a separate way to find healing before they come back together. As I went through blame, guilt and a host of dark emotions I never knew I could feel, I began to learn that I could stand on my own two feet and find peace. I learned that I was responsible for my own emotions and that the art of emotional detachment is sometimes necessary for survival.

Rather than taking on her husband's destructive energy and following him down a path of desolation, this courageous woman put her energy into nurturing her spiritual and personal development, taking classes, making new friends, enjoying life's simple pleasures, going for walks, and learning to love her own company. With time, she emerged more confident and in love with her own life than she ever dreamed possible.

*Soul Mate God of Limitless Possibilities, there are two kinds of aloneness: the kind that makes us feel thrown off the planet into solitary oblivion by trauma…and the kind that, after a deep breath, brings us strength and comfort. Thank you, God, for not abandoning soul mates who lose each other for a time.*

# Ships That Pass in the Night

*Every word of God proves true;*
*he is a shield to those who take refuge*
*in him.*

Proverbs 30:5

**T**he strains and joys of raising a young family and keeping up with community and employment responsibilities became too much for a young mother one holiday season. "My husband felt the same way," she says, "and eventually, exhaustion caused us to disconnect from each other." This sense of distance continued for some time until finally, near tears, the woman wrote her husband the following letter:

> Honey, as I write, I'm thinking of the cliché "being lonesome in a crowd." With our young and growing troop, I have a sneaky suspicion that both you and I have been feeling the same way but not voicing it. Am I right? Life is so busy right now that I sometimes feel you and I end up being two ships passing in the night as we guard our fleet of "little ships." We've both been so tired lately; it seems like we just end up shouldering our own separate worlds and duties as best we can, while the intimacy between us as best friends and partners gets filed for a later date.

I wish we could take a few deep breaths and try to find each other again. We used to talk about so many things: life, joys, accomplishments, sorrows and, most of all, what we thought God was doing in our lives. I just want to shout, "I miss that! I miss you!" I feel incomplete and hollow when we're not "us."

I don't want to prepare for Christmas, Honey, without sharing it with you. That's why I'm writing you this letter: to tell you how sorry I am that I haven't been able to be there for you lately and, while we both may feel like leaky boats, maybe we can help each other patch the leaks. I'm sorry for the times I've seemed picky or petty; that's what happens to me when I feel like we're not communicating and connecting.

Here we both are—loncly—and all we really want is each other and a big hug. I can't think of a better way to start Advent, what do you say?

Signed,
Mrs. Lonesome

The woman saved this letter because it represents a timeless message of tender, growing-up days that taught a lesson she never wants to forget: pulling together and connecting does not happen by accident. "We learned to lean on each other in ways we never knew were possible," she says. "Our renewed determination and commitment melded our relationship, and we found that heartache can deepen love rather than destroy it. We don't allow ourselves to be ships passing in the night. We care too much to let that happen for very long."

This woman admits that her marriage is scarred. There were times when she felt as if she were bleeding within from feeling used up, unappreciated and misunderstood. She knows that there were times when her husband felt the same way. "But life has taught us that we have to work at what is most important," she maintains. "Ongoing effort and vigilance is what keeps our fleet afloat."

*God of Ships and Partners That Pass in the Night, remind us that it doesn't have to be that way.*

# Double Blessings

*I stand in awe, O LORD, of your work.*
*In your own time revive it;*
*in our own time make it known.*

Habakkuk 3:2

"**S**ometimes, life seemed like one giant grindstone," wrote one woman. "Get up in the morning. Wade through soul-sucking demands all day. Come home. Crash. Fall into bed—and let duty drive you into the next day and the next. Do this, do that, shoulder this, shoulder that. Raised for duty from the time I was little, and after years of living an unbalanced life, I had a magnificent midlife crisis. It was the best thing that could have happened to me because I had to reevaluate why I found life so narrow, drudging and lusterless."

When duty becomes a flat, dreary way of existence, instead of the "blesser" and "joy-bringer" it is meant to be, we all need *perspective wideners*. Many years ago, I had an experience that reminded me of that very thing.

Although it was one of the hottest, most miserable days of the summer, my family and I drove to a nearby town to watch the Fourth of July fireworks. The humidity was so high it caused our shirts to stick like glue to our backs and, because there was no breeze, the mosquitoes were merciless. I'd had an exhausting day and I remember thinking, "I left home for this?"

Later, however, I wrote in my diary:

As the evening grew dim, the light waned and I could recognize friends only by voice as we all congregated expectantly on lawn chairs, blankets, car hoods and the prickly grass. Noses in the air, we waited for the drama to unfold while an unusual peach-colored full moon provided the perfect backdrop.

Suddenly, catching us off guard, the first display went off and the crowd released an "aaahhh," followed by an awestruck hush and then more loud exclamations. Each display was judged instanta- neously. "Look, it's a starfish. Look, it's like Christmas!" children cried in delight. The grand finale of music, lights, spirals and exploding colors was breathtaking. Then suddenly, it was over and we were collectively thrust back into the silent darkness of an ordinary, summer night. It was time to go home, put on the air conditioner, and return to reality.

But as we were driving home in the car, I kept glancing at the night sky, remembering the splendor we'd seen.

When I was a child in the 1950s—before there was such things as seat-belt safety consciousness—I used to curl up on the ledge of the back window of our old family car late at night when we motored home from going somewhere. I would lie looking up at the night sky, drowsing as I listened to the murmur of Mom and Dad talking in tones too soft for me to hear. I felt secure and enfolded, as if goodness and happiness would carry and surround me all my life. As a child, I sensed instinctively that the universe was a mothering, caring, magical place in which to live. As my breath fogged the window and I felt the coolness of the glass against the length of my body wrapped in a blanket, the endless star-speckled night would glimmer through the back window, teaching me that the cosmos is an intimate, personal world as close to me as the vapor on the window.

That night after the fireworks, I thought, "Why in the world would anyone ever allow the duties of everyday living to smother this life-giving truth?" The idea seemed preposterous, and I felt filled with compassion for the child in each of us who needs to believe when the adult in us is too overwhelmed or used up to care or remember.

*Universe God Who Sets Us Early upon Your Knee, the first lesson you teach is that awe is our birthright. Duty as a blesser and joy-bringer is only another form of this multifaceted dimension.*

# The Colors of Our Days

*"Their eyes see every precious thing."*
Job 28:10

Along time ago, when our boys were young, my husband and I took them for a trek around our village and to the cemetery beyond. I can remember the day clearly, because I had been feeling overwhelmed with housework.

The sky that day was an unusual gray-white, hinting of rain, and the yellow-green willow by the old gas station danced with the wind. I recall, too, hearing the voice of the wind racing fiercely through the crevices of old, abandoned buildings along Main Street.

The town seemed nearly deserted that day. As we sipped sodas on the post office steps, my husband, our boys and I watched the small walls of dust sweeping down the graveled side road. In that moment, I think we all sensed a certain communion and belonging with a time and people gone by. I remember saying to myself, "I can feel the ghosts among us," as my soul began to breath in wonder and forget about the duties at home that could wait.

As we walked out to the small cemetery a half mile south of town, the sun broke through the haze of the day and cast an odd, yellowish hue all around us. The boys, chattering and asking questions all along the way, collected stones and filled their pockets to bulging—as children will do. When we got to the cemetery, we stood on the grassy hill under the gnarled tree, letting the wind tear at our clothing and whip our hair across our faces. As the boys trotted among the grave markers, they read aloud the names and dates, calling, "Hey Dad, how old was this guy when he died?" Together, we thought of all the untold stories of people who had lived and walked in the very same places we did, noting that some of the markers dated back to as early as 1841.

When it was time to leave, the boys placed a few wildflowers on the graves of a baby and a nine-year-old boy who died in 1911, with whom the boys seemed to feel a special connection. These graves were hidden under an overgrown lilac bush, and the boys, enchanted by mystery, named them the Secret Graves. I remember watching the boys running their fingers over those two white-washed headstones with the lambs on top, reverently touching the spidery script with their small fingers.

My memories of that day are wrought with color; I can remember it like it was yesterday. It was as if the experience had moved inside me, like a painting on the wall of my soul.

Now that our children are grown, I realize how short the season of "childhood" is, how quickly our children move from their playful youth and enter that seemingly much longer season of "adulthood."

Today, the colors of my days are different—for this is

another season for me, too. Now, I have all the time in the world to clean house—but no little boys to put down for naps, to read to, or to ride a bike with. I say as many older mothers say, "I wish I had been less preoccupied. I wish I had cleaned the house less." Why did it seem so important?

*God of Young Mothers Who Grow Old, teach us what is precious at the time it is precious. When memories are inner paintings in the making, let us recognize and live the experience with relish—in the season it is happening, before it becomes the golden dust of the past.*

# A Mother's Calling

*As a mother comforts her child,*
*so I will comfort you.*

Isaiah 66:13

When teens become troubled and hard to reach, many mothers blame themselves, feeling as if they have somehow failed as a parent. One single mother, whose son had been in and out of alcohol and drug rehabilitation, said tearfully, "Sometimes, I can't read my own son. I can't tell what he is thinking. I don't seem to know when he needs to be left alone and when he is lonely and in need of encouragement." Although she would try to be sensitive to her son's moods, she sensed that he would get testy if she probed: "I feel mostly that he wants me to stay in the background of his life…so that's what I try to do on the small stuff. But I know that there are times when I have to be tough and stay in the picture. We've had some terrible fights when I have had to say no or insist he face the consequences for messes he's gotten himself into. And I get angry when he seems unwilling to meet me half way." This mother admits that she had to learn the hard way that "being a mother comes before being a friend…and that sometimes, even most times, our children think of us as the bad guy."

Another frustrated mother, whose young adult daughter had trouble keeping a job, taking responsibility and managing her finances, agreed. After years of feeling disrespected and disconnected from her daughter, the mother simply felt like giving up. "Sometimes I did," she confessed. "We had little in common, no similar passions. There just was so much distance between us." This mother, however, offers the secret to parenting: "But caring always drove me back. After all, we don't always get to be friends to our children, even though that might be what we'd prefer. Despite this, I know that God asks us to be Keepers of the Flame, the glow from which can be seen a long way off. Even if their backs are turned, our children will always know it's there."

*God Who Connects the Disconnected, when we feel like failures, remind us that a mother's commission is not to be perfect but to stand by. There is an ocean between giving up and having the wisdom to let go of certain unrealistic hopes and dreams.*

# No Gift Like a Sister

*How sweet is your love, my sister.*
Song of Solomon 4:10

The following words were written by a woman who was celebrating the reconciled relationship she shared with her sister:

> She loves people; I'm a loner. She's an indoor girl; I'm an outdoor girl. She follows Wall Street; I follow art and theater. She thrives on activity; I thrive on peace and quiet. She appreciates opera and church; I appreciate jazz and nature. She is Martha; I am Mary.
>
> Although I'm a redhead and my sister is a bottle blonde, we both have brown, expressive eyes. We love dogs, romantic movies, gaudy jewelry, hot peppers and Mexican food. We hate bowling and dieting. There's only a year between us, so we grew up sharing a bedroom, clothes, and the Hippie era and all the things that went with it. We both married tall men, had two children, and gradually grew apart as we had less and less in common. Our parents divorced, dividing our loyalties rather than drawing us closer. Eventually, we lost touch for a while, except for Christmas and birthday cards.

There seems to have been a serious falling out between these sisters at some time, but as the years passed they simply allowed time—rather than communication—to smooth things out. When something serious happened to one of them, the other never knew how much she was needed because they weren't sharing their lives. Fear of judgment and the risk of not being understood were obstacles they could not seem to rise above.

For a long time, words did not work for these women; rather, when they talked, things actually got worse. So they let the gift of time smooth out the wrinkles, substituting a platonic but safe-feeling relationship that began to work for both of them.

Throughout their differences, however, these women never lost respect for each other nor the mutual treasure of their many childhood memories. Eventually, the growing-apart times faded as loyalty and roots wove them back together. Today, these women are best friends as well as sisters—and they wish all sisters could have such a happy evolution. Their advice:

It's not what you have or don't have in common that counts but the ability to accept differences with unconditional caring, to let go of expectations of who each thinks the other should be, and to step over disappointments that happen in any relationship. Don't expect sisters to be perfect. Expect a certain amount of rivalry or lack of synchronicity. Expect ups and downs. Expect one step forward and two steps backward. Give each other space. Keep in touch. Forgive, forget, laugh. Back off when you need to. Be your own person. Meet each other where you're at.

Tolerate shortcomings and differences of opinions. Hold hands when you need to. Remember that if something happened to your sister, a part of you would die, too. *There is no gift like a sister.*

*God Who Knits Harmony into the Lives of All Sisters—whether estranged or not, whether ideas and passions match or not—nothing matters as long as their souls love.*

# Last Gift

*"Return to your home."*

Luke 8:39

others and daughters sometimes come to know each other late in life. "I have always been a private, reserved person both by nature and because of the era I grew up in," shared one woman. "I was married in the late 1940s. When my daughter was an adult, she said, 'Mother, sometimes, I've felt as if I never really knew you.' It hurt me to hear her say that. I didn't know how to respond because I've never been comfortable sharing my feelings." Soon after this conversation with her daughter, the woman was diagnosed with cancer and died. Her story, though, has a happy ending.

Before she died, this woman shared how she and her daughter were able to express their love for each other:

Life did not turn out the way I'd planned. We never had much money, and I always felt a lot of stress and anxiety when my children were growing up. I kept my feelings to myself, though, not realizing that in my attempts to spare them worry I never let the joy show either. I was enmeshed in taking care of the family, attending to my daily chores, and trying to hold everything together when I felt exhausted. The years slipped away, and it seems I never did find time for myself. Now that I am dying, the gift of time has come to me.

I have written a letter to my daughter and left it in her recipe file, where I am certain she will find it. It reads: "I am so sorry you have felt as if you don't know me. I, too, have felt as if I didn't know me. I remember so many golden times when you were growing up; how proud I was of you. I never realized that you didn't know. I was often unsure of myself, simply trying to find the courage to meet each day's many demands. I should have sat on the bed with you and chatted into the night. I should have strolled under the moonlight with you, taken you for a walk in the rain. I should have asked you many things and told you many things—but how could I teach you what I didn't know myself? Times were so much different then from what they are now.

"Being close to you now in these last days, seeing you and being with you, means so much to me. You know I have never been one for a lot of words, but I want you to know that your mother has come home to herself. It is my last gift to you, to be able to tell you that I have found and know myself after all these years. Beauty and strength fill my days, and I am at peace. I feel as if I am sinking into deep, velvet folds. The deeper I sink, the more I relive our days together. In my mind, I touch your hand, blow dandelion fluff with you, tell you enchanting stories, lie in the grass and watch clouds with you—for time is now still. There are no worries to consume me; there are no distractions or fears to keep us from knowing each other. I am my real self at last, and the fullness of my love for you carries me as it always has.

"I want these to be my last words to you—for you to feel that you know me in the language of the heart, that my love will always reach beyond the grave."

*God of Mothers and Daughters, when you call us home, be it to ourselves, each other, or heaven, it is always, always possible to find the way.*

# Red Ball of Trust

*But I trust in you, O L*ORD*,*
  *I say, "You are my God."*
*My times are in your hand.*

Psalm 31:14–15

When women's dreams fall apart, they often tumble with a resounding crash resembling the splintering collapse of a demolished building. The echoing sounds of our destroyed dreams leave an aching clamor in our heart as we sit in the surrounding rubble, sifting idly through the dust and wondering if anything is salvageable. Tears of sorrow sting our eyes, and sometimes we feel angry, perhaps blaming God for the fact that our heartfelt plans did not materialize. Following the collapse of a treasured dream, one woman wrote:

> I became cold and very hard to reach, but eventually, as light breaks through storm clouds, insight seemed to filter through my mind. I realized how pre-occupation with my ideas and dreams had mush-roomed out of control. I had lacked trust that God would care enough about my passion to build my dream with me. When everything fell apart, I realized how little I had sought spiritual guidance, how little I had prayed, how little I had let God in.

This woman began to do image work, trying to understand what went wrong. In her imagination, a scenario took place, with trust represented by a big red ball and with God as guardian of the universe:

In my mind, I sat on the floor clinging to my big, red ball, grasping it tightly to my chest and defiantly saying, "Mine, mine!" God, wearing a flowing robe, stood only a few feet away, but I would not look up. Then I heard a gentle voice say, "Give me the ball," and I saw hands reaching out toward me, but I only clung tighter to the ball. "No," I insisted. "I can't. I won't!" Then I saw the hands drop away and the folds of the robe settle on the floor beside me. I realized that God had dropped to my level and was sitting quietly beside me, not saying anything. I knew in my heart that God was asking for my trust.

Sometimes, I don't know how to find peace in uncertainty. It is actually fear that holds me back. In this imagined scene, I relaxed my hold on the ball but rested my hand protectively over it to signify ownership. I looked at God openly, surprised to see the pain in my eyes reflected back to me. I then asked God, "How can I be sure you'll come through for me when I need you the most?"

There, in those words, I had finally voiced the ultimate question. I felt deeply sad, the ball lying unguarded on my knees, apparently unnoticed. In that moment, I told God the truth: that if I were to give up the ball, I would feel like I'd lost control of my affairs—meaning that I would have to meet the waves of hardship head on, that I would be asked to increase my spiritual stamina and multiply my compassion. I feared that saying yes to God meant saying yes to growth that could hurt—and I didn't feel I was ready for that. I felt I'd known enough pain. Yet, when I looked at the pile of rubble I had created by myself, I realized I wasn't doing so hot on my own.

This woman says that her fantasy meditation went on for hours as she wrestled with her thoughts:

I could feel God waiting, letting me weigh my thoughts. Loving patience seemed to envelope me as I mulled over an important decision: Was I going to cling to the measly trust I had in myself and in my own control, or was I going to offer my trust to God? I took my time, but I finally made a decision I have never regretted. In my imagination, I watched the ball slowly roll down my legs and bump softly onto the floor, until it finally came to rest within the folds of God's robe. "Are you sure?" I heard the gentle voice ask. Then, as God rested a caring hand upon the ball as if it were a precious object, I said, "Yes."

*Dream Builder God, when we rebuild our dreams through you, with you and in you, disappointment does not destroy us. Rather, wonders only you could imagine rise through the rubble as we put our trust in your hands.*

# One Final Poke

*"Out of the believer's heart shall flow rivers of living water."*

John 7:38

O ne woman was experiencing tremendous dissatisfaction at work as a result of a situation that was causing her to feel disregarded and unappreciated. Continually trying to go the extra mile to display her good intentions to be a team player, she was feeling exhausted and dispirited. The document she presented to her supervisors that respectfully stated her experience and asked for changes was met with not only rejection but a letter of reprimand. Shortly after the woman received this unexpected, harsh response, she had a powerful dream:

> I was in a river valley, but the water was barely trickling. Almost instinctively, I went to the source of the problem, where the water was blocked. I picked up a large stick and poked in the mud around the clogged area. Suddenly, with one final poke, the clogged area burst apart and the water flowed freely, rushing clearly and brightly down the riverbed and throughout the countryside. I had freed the river. The dream carries many symbolic undertones for me, representing the struggles in my psyche.

As author Denise Linn puts it, "Water is one of the most universal signs throughout the world. Though it varies in richness of meaning from culture to culture, it usually is connected to emotions, feelings, intuition, psychic perceptions and the subconscious mind, as well as the mysterious realms of the archetypal female energy....Flowing water can represent flowing emotions and feelings. Blocked or dammed water can mean that your feelings are blocked....Crystal clear water can symbolize clarity, being in tune with life around you and connected to the inner feminine energy of receptivity and intuition. Stagnant water can mean you are stuck emotionally and it's time to shift gears, to step out of your emotional quagmire....This is your unconscious self, the waters of life, the source of your vitality."

The woman continues to evaluate her life and consider creative alternatives, including possible employment changes. It is an unsettling time for her because she is questioning her place in life. Should she stay or should she go? Should she wait the problem out or is it time to move on? She remains attuned to her spiritual path, values the advice of friends, pays attention to unfolding events and ideas, and doesn't discount the discernment of her own heart. She believes that in time the right thing will make itself known. This wise woman will not rush into a quick-fix solution that doesn't really address the deeper issues, but at the same time she is not going to tolerate an unendurable situation indefinitely.

*God Who Frees Rivers and People, sometimes we stop trying, believing and trusting…just one poke shy of the one that would break through the problem, opening up whole new worlds of possibilities in our lives.*

# Old Wounds

*For a twofold grief possessed them,*
*and a groaning at the memory of what*
*had occurred.*

Wisdom of Solomon 11:12

O ne woman writes a letter to God when she needs to talk about something that is troubling her. In her letter, she freely pours out her thoughts and emotions, without concern for punctuation and grammar. When she finishes her letter to God, she waits several minutes and then writes the letter she thinks God would return to her. This simple exercise, a form of written prayer, helps this woman gain perspective and peace. She shares the following letters about a particularly bad time:

> Oh God, it's been a really rotten time. Nothing is going right, I feel overwhelmed, spread too thin, scattered and unable to focus on what is important. I truly regret how some things have turned out recently—things I didn't do and should have done for my family. I am distracted, done in and unable to get my attitude above wishy-washy, which is usually out of character for me. I know you are aware of all these burdens I'm carrying right now, but it always helps to talk them out with you. I sense that you draw close as I write, saying to me, as you always do, "Let's start at

the beginning."

Well, God, it seems I was doing great for quite a while—then something happened, a "kick-in-the-teeth" kind of thing, and I was thrown into a really bad space where a universe of bad memories just waited to grab at me. Ever since that time, I've been feeling defeated, weak, sorry for myself, lonely, sad. I feel I have had to carry far more than my share of conflicts...and that just doesn't seem fair. When I feel like this, God, all I can think about is how much I deserve a break, how unfair it is that I have to deal with so much. I want to know what I've done to deserve such treatment. Isn't that a fair question, God?

After reading over her letter to God and sitting with her thoughts and emotions for several minutes, this woman turned her attention to the letter that God might send to her in response. She imagined God writing:

Dear Daughter, you're doing fine. You think that because an old wound haunts you from time to time that you aren't healed, haven't grown, haven't moved forward. You have. You've not done anything wrong. You keep thinking you've failed somehow but you haven't. You feel shame, as if somehow you haven't measured up, proved yourself or been strong enough—simply because your memories continue to hurt. Just remember this: Healing is not about forgetting. Deep wounds to the heart become a part of the inner psyche, and unexpected conversations or incidents can trigger old memories. When that happens, tell yourself these things:

"The inner work I am doing is healthy and healing."
"There's nothing more I can do."
"The many earnest efforts I've made are enough."
"I have the right to inner peace."
"I have the right to be my true and best self."
"I do not need to defend myself."

This woman is able to find her own wisdom deep within when she brings her concerns to God in her letter-writing prayer. She is renewed in soul and spirit, ready to be all she wants to be for herself and her family.

*Soother of Wounds, just because a wound is still imprinted in our memory bank does not mean that it has power any longer to hurt us. Bad memories are empty husks of the past that rattle in the wind when our lives move on to the wondrous things God has planned for us.*

# Night Prayers

Night is a realm unto itself. It's a time that calls us to shift our rhythm from the hectic bustle of our daylight hours to the slower, simpler pace of the evening.

Night is also, as Denise Linn writes, "the realm of the feminine principle. It is the domain of dreams, ancient mysteries and our subconscious mind." It is a time to quiet our inner world so we can avail ourselves of the spiritual power and consolation that is the essence of human rest. One woman disciplined herself to include bedtime meditation as part of her evening routine. She explains her experience in this way:

> The quiet of the night brings peace to my soul. The sacrifice of foregoing sleep sweetens the silence as I sit alone before God. I tell myself there is no responsibility that can't wait until morning. The household is at rest and so, too, is my soul. The warm darkness, the total lack of sound and commotion soothes my weary spirit. I intentionally focus on laying aside tomorrow to be with God in the hours of night. Slowly, the tranquillity that only communion

with God can bring descends upon me, and I find that God is in the silence. My heartbeat slows as my body relaxes and, although I yearn to close my eyes and sleep, a soft voice says, "No, stay awake. Say your prayers."

Briefly—only briefly—I spill out my frustrations and concerns. After all, words spoil the surrender. They make waves in the fragile serenity that descends in the quiet. I usually gaze at a particular cross as I sit curled in a wing chair. The face of the plaster figure of Christ on that cross is crushed beyond recognition—and I will never repair it. The brokenness of it touches me and makes me feel protective. It reminds me, too, of my own brokenness, but I do not dwell on my shortcomings. I know God knows, and that is all that matters. I simply let the words "Let it rest" circle repetitively through my mind. And then I do just that; I let it rest.

As I take deep, slow breaths and allow God to erase the clinging cobwebs of busyness from my mind, my taut nerves relax and I begin to sink even deeper into my chair. If I could see my face, I know that it would look smoother and free of lines. My mind becomes like a flower that opens only at night—and I feel it responding to God's call and touch. I often wonder why I can't be like that during the day, why I let commotions, duties and responsibilities get the best of me. But these questions only bring back the tension. So when they arise I slowly fold my hands, close my eyes, and repeat my mantra: Let it rest. The last thing I remember is the stillness of surrender as my consciousness slips into soothing places beneath my jittery nerves and the memories of the day's stress.

*God of Flowers That Bloom in the Night, when we fall asleep in prayer, the tightness of the day drops away without our even knowing it. Our souls always know the difference.*

# Righteous Rage

*As fire consumes the forest*
*    as the flame sets the mountains ablaze,*
*so pursue them with your tempest....*
*Fill their faces with shame.*
                        Psalm 83:14-15,16

L ike a tidal wave of hot lava spilling from a volcano and destroying everything in its path, rage can sweep over us women with devastating power, leaving our hands shaking and our hearts racing. If left unchecked, rage leaves us standing on a precipice of feelings that can threaten to wreak havoc in all areas of our lives.

One professional woman frequently experiences this rush of rage in her working environment. While friendly banter exists in the offices of the prestigious legal firm where she works, she is painfully aware of the subtle hierarchy of power—of which she occupies a lower rung. She wrote:

I must stand up for equality regarding what I earn, and I have to defend the amount of time I spend with clients. The basic motto of the firm is to spend as little time as possible with clients while at the same time increasing billable hours as much as possible.

My career is important to me. I love what I do and care deeply about the people I help. I am an intelligent, reasonable woman—and I understand the value of compromise in the business world. But sometimes the injustice of the male-dominated, patriarchal perspective infuriates me. When I feel patronized, insulted or not taken seriously one time too many, I feel like a volcano that could erupt. My rage is not only for myself but against the inequality I see around me, in the world and in my community. I am by nature a caretaker, born with the heart of an activist. My passion lies with the downtrodden, the disadvantaged, women and children, the voiceless and the common people.

Sometimes this woman wants to cry, "What is wrong with you people? Why can't you get it? Why does there have to be a hierarchy, winners and losers, a separation of classes?" She feels these things strongly, but she also knows in her heart that too much protest will make her physically, emotionally and spiritually ill.

Gathering in, regrouping and recovering from a bad spell is never easy for this woman, but she knows she needs to do it if she is to preserve her integrity. "I must cool the fires within for my own sake and the causes I care about so that I can carry on and be effective," she asserts. For her, the bottom line is just that: carrying on, motivated by her passionate belief in her life's work.

*God of Justice, fighting fire with fire is not always the answer. Channeled rage can be a gift. When we temper it with a cool head, the power to cope and affect change doubles.*

# Queens of Charity

*Your throne, O God, endures forever
    and ever.
    Your royal scepter is a scepter of equity;
    you love righteousness....
At your right hand stands the queen in
    gold of Ophir.*

Psalm 45:6-7, 9

It is part of the female experience to feel, from time to time, that we aren't accepted for who and what we are. This is an especially painful experience when we women make a concentrated effort to do our best or contribute our finest and it seems to go unappreciated or misunderstood. We often feel like giving up and embracing the motto, "What's the use? I'm through trying." One woman wrote:

> I finally let bitterness wash over me from head to foot, and my heart felt blackened, like the inside of an ill-kept chimney. I felt I'd tried and tried and tried...but nothing seemed to make a difference; I was always on the outside looking in. When I found out that another woman had made a cruel, cold-hearted, untrue remark about me, it was like the last straw. "She's not fit to shine my shoes," I concluded, allowing feelings of hatred and thoughts of revenge pour through me.

Ironically, though, as time went on, I found a gift. I became stronger and more sure of myself as a direct result of that betrayal. I realized that truth is truth and others cannot take that from me or cause me to feel inferior no matter what they think. When I came home to my own worth, I no longer felt the need to prove myself—and there is no greater freedom than that.

Another woman, who was also working to overcome bitterness wrote:

Not talking about it was the worst. When I finally poured out my feelings to my daughter-in-law, who is also a good friend, I realized that feeling rejected was at the core of my bitterness. As we talked, I realized that although my feelings of bitterness certainly were valid as far as what had transpired was concerned, being bitter was not how I wanted to be in life. Three words then came to me as we were talking: "safety," "healing" and "charity." Safety referred to knowing that I could safely pour out my thoughts to my daughter-in-law, who would respect them and keep them in confidence. The healing was a healing of perspective that occurred when I expressed the truth about how I felt and who I wanted to be.

Charity, however, is the most significant of the three words. It implied a greatness of spirit that I knew to be at the heart of goodness. When I was a girl, I used to think that charity meant being willing to be walked on like a door mat—not standing up for yourself or always turning the other cheek as a gesture of humility or goodness. As I became an experienced woman, I put away such misguided foolishness and adopted a term I call "Queens of Charity." Queens of Charity stand tall, walk straight, listen well, speak their minds, and do not bend to pettiness or narrow thinking. They are nurturing when they need to be and fierce when love and forgiveness call for it. They do not put on airs, and they do not shrink from betrayal. Even when bruised to the bone, Queens of Charity move forward, sustained by inner confidence, gentleness and faith in better days.

*God of Feminine Power and Authority, women who rule their lives with the fire of charity in their hearts shine with the fulfillment of the promise of your Holy Spirit within.*

# An Old Lady's Legacy

*From the womb of the morning
like dew, your youth will come to you.*
                                    Psalm 110:3

**T**oo often our culture overlooks the beauty of an aging woman. Yet age can be a woman's crowning glory and goodness. One woman wrote the following essay about her great-aunt:

> Whenever I was feeling that life was trickier than I'd like, a visit with my great-aunt always left me feeling reflective, softer and more kindly toward the seasons in my own life. If my husband and I were experiencing a lot problems in our relationship or gray hair was coming in or crows feet were developing around my eyes or I was just feeling old in spirit, my great-aunt's positive nature always inspired me to try to enjoy life, to seek the golden moments, to nurture others, and to appreciate honest, hard work as a gift.
>
> My great-aunt used to refer to her past as the "days of wine and roses." A widow for a number of years, she lived alone in the house her beloved husband built for her when they were newlyweds. A look

of sheer tenderness always crossed her face when she spoke his name, and I wanted to look away from her in honor of the intimacy of her private thoughts. The moment would pass, though, and she would faintly say, "And that's life. One must go on." She was not sad, though. Her mind would simply drift, for only a moment, to a place deep and faraway that only she could visit.

Whenever I spent time with my great-aunt, she always showed me old black-and-white photos of her family, all the while tracing her fingers over the portraits like a caress. She spoke with delight of the old days: playing cards, visiting neighbors, riding around in Model T Fords, and dancing the night away in filmy silk dresses and wearing Evening in Paris cologne. Even at ninety-four, the soft shadows of her youthful beauty lingered in her eyes and smile.

Being allowed to visit the past with my great-aunt never failed to make me more determined to experience life more fully and to seek the naturalness and simplicity of the faith that she exhibited. Disillusioned with religion, I sat with her in church many times, my thoughts scattered and complicated, while her lips moved silently and reverently in prayer. I will never forget her sincerity, humility or zest for life.

My great-aunt's fine house is empty since her death a week ago, but her tailored clothes still hang in the closets, her plants still flower with life, and the worn piano sits in the corner awaiting her touch. Through her passing, I have come to see that living a life of faith is a good thing, that the love between a man and a woman can transcend time and space, and that growing old can be a blessing.

*God of Wine and Roses, we have much to look forward to, in both this life and the next.*

# Arm in Arm

*Nor did their own arm give them victory,*
*but your right hand, and your arm,*
*and the light of your countenance,*
*for you delighted in them.*

Psalm 44:3

**B**eyond the strength and value of a woman's autonomy lies the sisterhood of others who are also embracing life, healing from scars, and transforming their lives. Arm in arm, as a "community of the wounded," women are created to sojourn together.

One woman who turned forty wrote:

Midlife for me brought a gathering in, not only of myself but of the activities and friendships in my life. I found myself letting go of some relationships as I simplified my life and, for the first time, understood the spirituality of minimalism. I found I could not be all things to all people, that I simply did not have the capacity to be there for certain people. I could not and would not be able to please everyone.

What grief and confusion that phase of life was for me! I actually had nightmares about not being present to people I felt were counting on me (when, in fact, they did not need me as much as I thought). It's a bit humorous now, but moving beyond being a "people pleaser" was actually traumatic for me. I was always worried that someone would get mad at me or wouldn't like me anymore.

This woman began to trust that if she couldn't be there for others, God could...and would. With this realization came a new strength and clarity that brought her great peace. When she understood her womanhood as being one pair of arms, she learned that she could embrace God, life and others with passion but that there are limits to how far one pair of arms can realistically reach. "I believe we are all called to service as our highest privilege," she insists, "but serving others does not mean pleasing everyone. I think this is the wisest and most powerful lesson I ever learned. It was also the most painful."

*God Who Can Be All Things to All People, when women stand shoulder to shoulder and arm in arm, love girds the globe and no one is ever left out. Could it be that simple?*

# Woman-Images

*Open my eyes, so that I may behold
    wondrous things....
You enlarge my understanding.*

Psalm 119:18, 32

Following a lengthy hardship experience, I came to realize that revelations usually take place gradually, not all at once. With that understanding, I could see my life in images, as if a cosmic artist were at work painting and creating me as my life unfolded. Yet there is no discernible master plan for me—rather, there is a sense that God is waiting with me as I become myself.

Despite the wonder and reassurance of this realization, however, I continued to have difficulty with inner scars, feeling as if life had trapped me at the bottom of a well from which I simply could not emerge. Then, in my periods of meditation, I began imagining various woman-images that called me into healing.

At first, I imagined a tall woman I named The Strand Gatherer—the one who taught me to gather in, honor and embrace my experiences. I used her image on the cover of my first book.

Then I had a vision of The Well Woman. Her very body is

a well, with her arms reaching out and up to encircle the top of the well. This image helped me imagine *myself* as a well. For me, this self-image carried with it an encouraging message: *You are never* in *a well, you* are *a well. Draw deeply from the waters of faith.*

When a friend explained that surrendering to our troubles does not mean giving up—as I was unconsciously fearing—but rather *opening up*, I found myself imaging yet another woman, this one shriveled and covered with scars from head to toe. I did not find this woman ugly, though, but merely herself. I called her Resurrected Woman. There was an ancient knowing about her, and I felt that I wanted to protect her. In my imagination, I stayed with that image and watched as her outer, physical framework fell away, like a snakeskin, to reveal a new spirit that rose out of her scars with great strength and wisdom.

Soon after this, I found what I considered to be my most significant woman-image. This one came in three images of a single bridge. First I saw a woman with her arms outstretched, embracing and holding a bridge across her ample breast. Then I saw her very arms and hands become the bridge itself, which she extended across a deep chasm. Finally, I saw her lay her body across the chasm, where it was transformed into a bridge across which people and animals could safely cross. I call this image Bridge Woman of Safe Passage. To me, she represents the world's need for human beings who are willing to do four things: open, deepen, transform and heal their lives so that they might become bridges of safety across spiritual, political and personal chasms.

Psychologists call these images archetypes. To me, they are simply love-inspired woman-images that weave beauty and truth into our lives when we open our hearts.

*Multi-Faceted God Who Reveals Our Potential, we can only begin to imagine the height, the width and the breadth of the wonder we are called to be.*

# A Flood of Tears

*God made a wind blow over the earth, and the waters subsided; the fountains of the deep and the windows of the heavens were closed, the rain from the heavens was restrained, and the waters gradually receded from the earth.*

Genesis 8:1-3

Years ago, raging floods swept through our village countryside and my family's beloved woods. Our footpaths were obliterated as if a giant broom had swept them away, leaving behind nothing more than a floor of slick, smooth mud. Grief-stricken, I set out to discover the damages—and the changes.

As I walked through the woods that day, a sharp wind suddenly came up, rushing through the tree tops and making them bend and bow with a force they could not hold steady against. At ground level, however, I felt nothing more than a slight breeze, as if God were reaching supple, caring arms around me, protecting me from the wind's force.

As I walked even deeper into the woods, I noticed that Dead Tree Gulch was swollen beyond recognition, its brown, glassy surface still except for mysterious ripples and spirals. An immense, nearly submerged log near the shore reminded me of a lurking primeval creature, its smell pungent and swamp-like. At one point, I sunk to my knees in the mud and had to clamor to find solid ground. Suddenly, finding my footing, I broke through to a small area where the old, familiar path remained intact. Even there, though, the ravages of the flood were evident in the litter of trash snagged among fallen branches and tree roots. Surveying the power of the flood sobered me as I encountered another shocking sight; across the path lay a three-hundred-pound railroad tie that had been swept off its foundation half a block away, carried along in the flood waters to come to rest here in the woods.

Standing there feeling surrounded by destruction, I found at my feet a small measure of evidence that offered the first signs of returning life: the tracks of a deer. I also noticed the water marks on nearby trees, indicating that the waters had, at one time, been over six feet above my head. I realized that it would take years but the woods would eventually reclaim itself as the hallowed, peaceful place it had always been, providing home and shelter for plants and wildlife and welcoming the tread of human feet seeking solace.

When our seventeen-year-old son died by probable suicide, I—like the woods—was ravaged by a force that hurled a three-hundred-pound railroad tie into my heart. For weeks, I had panic attacks, nightmares without ceasing and dread that filled my every waking moment. Riddled with channels of doubt and fear, I did not think I would survive those weeks. Vast shorelines in my inner being seemed to have caved in from savage floods of grief, and I was sure I would never know peace again.

Eventually, however, I began to notice some "deer tracks" in the mud below my feet. I found I could go on—at first an hour at a time, then an afternoon and, finally, an entire day. I began to realize that I could—and did—believe in the life of the spirit. Like that time in the woods when the winds encircled the trees, I found that I could feel God's tender embrace sheltering me with love, only I now felt my son in that same embrace.

*God of Ancient Floods That Sweep the Human Heart, life insists on continuance. For the ravaged, the first signs of returning life begin with tiny tracks of courage. Let us not miss those tracks that lead us to the faith and confidence that will take us where we need to go.*

# Ten Lessons

*I have a hope in God...that there will be a resurrection.*

Acts 24:15

**M**ost women are not trained in the "spirituality of horror." We do not plan for those experiences—a tragic death, a horrible accident, an unexpected or unwanted divorce, an incurable disease—that broadside us like a monsoon, body-slamming us with terror and sweeping out to sea every foundation we depended upon. The initial impact of horror is the shock of trying to comprehend what has hit us.

At the moment of Jesus' death, the curtain in the sanctuary was torn in two, and that is how we feel—as if the veil of protection in our lives has been ripped in half. And herein lies the *first lesson:* You lose your sense of security forever. With this lesson comes post-traumatic stress that sears like bolts of lightening. You learn that there is no emotion "inappropriate" or "abnormal," that nightmares, the inability to sleep, and the feelings of depression and despondency are simply part of your daily life.

Then, as you become well acquainted with these companions, you learn the *second lesson*: You can tolerate all these feelings because you have to. They are now the landscape of your life-ravaged-by-trauma. You have, in effect, no choice.

The *third lesson* comes with the first tentative tendrils of exploring "why." How could this happen to you? But all you have are questions to which there are no answers. Which brings you to the *fourth lesson:* It's okay not to have answers.

More time passes, and by now you are at least acting normally and smiling in the right places when people talk to you. Grace somehow enables you to go through the motions. The first signs of comfort rise in your ability to function as you return to work, take on your routine responsibilities, and begin tending once again to those you care about. Without realizing it, you progress to the *fifth lesson:* Reaching out to others is life-giving and you are actually able to do it.

Gradually, greater comfort weaves its way into your life, but with it comes the *sixth lesson:* Setbacks will inevitably occur, probably for the rest of your life. You reel with the finality of the realization that your eyes may be dry but your heart continues to sob. You sink into the bleak truth that healing won't come without plunging into this transforming darkness.

By now, you know that no one can understand your journey. Those who have not known your particular horror have begun distancing themselves, and you realize that this is best. You begin gathering in and letting go, no longer needing to turn to exterior experiences. These helped at first, but now you learn the *seventh lesson:* Your horror will always be there. You sense, of course, that it will evolve, but you find peace only as you let go of "outcomes" and acquire the ability to embrace uncertainty and trust simultaneously.

*Lesson eight* brings you great knowledge: God will never again fit into a box; hope is going to find you, not the other way around; and learning to live with your horror is going to take a lifetime.

*Lesson nine* brings the wisdom of tenderness: Material things mean nothing to you; you only care about that which is eternal.

*Lesson ten* brings a promise that you wouldn't have believed before: Your horror has wounded you, but it has not destroyed you. Love *is* stronger than death. You feel the resurrection of that realization lifting you up and bringing you salvation every single day.

*God of Holy Thursday and Good Friday, only you can empathize when we feel as if our faith has been to hell and back again. Battered and shaken, we learn that resurrection is not some far-off, obscure happening but a living incarnation of comfort that is with us now, when we need it most.*

# Crystallization

*Then the angel showed me the river of the*
*water of life, bright as crystal, flowing from*
*the throne of God.*

Revelation 22:1

Unspeakable grief enters women's lives through many avenues: death, illness, divorce, abuse, addiction, painful relationships, injustices. A woman well-versed in heartbreak once wrote to a friend:

> Have you ever dropped a marble into a pot of boiling water to create those beautiful crackles throughout the clear crystal of the marble? That is how our hearts feel when we are immersed in severe pain. We feel we can't bear the plunge, that we are too fragile and could be easily broken and shattered. What we don't know is that there is a scientific name for the spiritual transformation process that is happening to us; it is called *crystallization*. It takes thousands of years for a crystal to be formed, which is why it is revered throughout the world for its transparency, purity and clarity. Unspeakable grief, over a long period of time, brings us similar gifts. At first, we don't want them, but later we come to understand how life-giving and valuable they are.

This woman's friend, herself knowing the gifts of crystallization that allowed her to reach out and help others, wrote back:

> Yes, the crackles inside us become like stretch marks that are evidence of past pain. I am reminded of a friend whose fourteen-year-old son was murdered. Her whole being screamed with grief and rage for a very long time, but that time has passed. She has healed, feels a deep closeness to her son's spirit, and has even written a book to help others. She still carries the stretch marks of that experience and misses her son, but she no longer feels that she cannot go on. She has found a way to be at peace.

Without the crystallization process, the fullness of time cannot heal; we cannot reclaim our ability to live and mold a vision of hope for our future. Writer Pat Samples describes this process well: "Stay in the moment. Each moment's grief by itself is enough to handle; anticipated or remembered grief is too much to bear. Stay anchored in the love from which your grief springs. Know that the love-grief is sculpting you into a raw and priceless wonder even as it cuts deep. Let loved ones who have passed over live on in you. Let them comfort you. They are not done blessing you. No matter what your grief, settle yourself into the reassuring arms of God."

*God of Solace, wrenching grief crystallizes into rivers of healing when we turn to you and each other. There is no other way and no greater wisdom than that wrought through crystallized pain.*

# The Soul of a Village

*I have seen this example of wisdom…and it seemed great to me. There was a little city with few people in it.*

Ecclesiastes 9:13-14

After recovering from a deep emotional wound, one woman found herself thinking about all the other women in her rural community and the hardships and sorrows they, too, had experienced. As she began to think of her small town as having a life and spirit of its own, she wondered what it would say. The following fable came to her:

> Long ago there was a little village who had once been a big town. Wistfully speaking with surrounding small towns, the little village said, "There's not much left of us now, is there? We were all once large and thriving cities—but now we're on the way out." Together, the little village and surrounding small towns sighed with regret and loss saying, "Yes, those were the days" and "Weren't we something!"
>
> Then, after much reflection, the little village said, "You know, I'm too tired to keep remembering. It doesn't matter anyway—and besides, I ache in all my bones. I think I'm going to sleep—it's just too

hard to keep going."

And with that, the little village fell into a deep slumber and, like a coverlet, Sister Winter came and fell across the village's shoulders. "Just rest, then," Sister Winter said, and the little village murmured in reply, "Cover me well and bring magic to my dreams."

With a flourish, Sister Winter brandished her crystal cloak, took up her staff, and began her vigil, guarding every back alley, every cracked walkway, and every nook and cranny of the little town. Snow, like diamond dust, feathered the town's stark trees and softened the edges on every aging building. And time passed.

As promised, Sister Winter filled the little town's dreams with magic: hot-yellow summers, loves and lovers, parades and big-band music, root beer floats, new pine lumber, the laughter of children, barking dogs, the scent of lilacs.

And then, at the end of forty days, Sister Winter appeared in the courts of Mother Time: "Mother, I have kept my vigil—but the little village is still evolving. She continues to think that losing her momentum means loosing her spirit." "Ah," said Mother Time, who never hurried with anything. Gradually, turning her attention from the solar systems, the planets, the comets and all the rest of the universe, Mother Time focused all her care on the little village slumbering in the mantle of Sister Winter—and smiled. "You may awaken the little village now, Sister," she declared.

The next morning, the little village awoke to sunshine and melting icicles and knew that something was different. The few remaining townspeople were gathering in the public square and smiling in satisfaction at the banner they had hung across Main Street. It read: Our Soul Is Still Growing. In smaller letters underneath the decree, they had written: "We are held by all that we were. The love, the lessons, the transformed hurt, the goodwill, the faith, the forgiveness, the courage, the tolerance, the memories all weave hope into our days. We have as much living to do as we ever did, only now our history and wisdom are holding out their hands *to us*."

*God Who Overlaps Past, Present and Future, how could we ever forget that we live, breathe and walk with shadows, shadings and voices gone before, just waiting to offer us consolation, strength and vision for living?*

# Faces beyond the Mirror

*For now we see in a mirror dimly, but then we shall see face to face.*

1 Corinthians 13:12

Women are deeply attuned to the passing of time and the movement of life from one generation to the next. Sometimes, in a quiet moment, we become aware of our female ancestors hovering in the shadows of our lives, companions to us in our own ongoing journeys.

One woman is especially aware of this when she looks into the mirror of her great-grandmother's old oak dresser, something she inherited years after her great-grandmother's death. Although the mirror's backing has been eaten away with time, leaving age spots that distort the image, the woman doesn't consider the mirror "damaged." She writes:

When I look in the mirror, I think of all the times my great-grandmother's face appeared in that looking glass as she pinned up her hair, clasped a broach at her throat, or smoothed on a bit of face powder. From where did she draw her strength? What was it like for her to cross the ocean to come to America from Norway? She died young, at the age of thirty-five; I myself am over a decade older than she was when she died. Did she ever wonder who her descendants would be? Was I ever a glimpse in her imagination? I like to think that I could have been, but of course that is a rather romantic notion.

Women carry with them this kind of kindred connection with other women. Some of us lie awake at night and wonder who will come after us. There, in the quiet, we feel the pain of the world—a world in trouble, besieged by war and famine, suffering from materialism and ecological atrocities—and we long to protect the children of our sons and daughters and their children. We yearn to extend the sound of our voices through time, into the years ahead, to gather in those who will be our descendants. For women, this is a sacred mission that comes from tapping into the deepest realms of God.

There is an unspoken language among women. It is found in the rustle of a breeze under a gauzy white curtain, in the brushing of tree branches against a roof on a stormy night, in the sounds of tiny tree frogs and crickets, in the splashing of children through friendly mud puddles. It is heard in the rhythmic creak of a rocking chair, the soft breath of a sleeping child, the snore of a beloved husband. It communicates through the smell of the sweaty hair of a little boy who has played in the sun all day. It rises from a young girl's first kiss, an old woman's pickle patch, a grandpa's shaving cream, the red cap on a bald baby.

To note and cherish these things is to be mindful of an ancient thread that binds all women who have lived before, who are now, and who will come in the future. When the woman looks into her great-grandmother's mirror and sees her own image, she wonders if someday her own great-granddaughter will wonder about her. She writes:

> As I pause to adjust an earring or smooth my hair, I feel such tender caring for the women who are my kinsfolk—the ones who came before me and the ones yet unborn. It is prayer at its best.

*God of Women Still to Come, let us never forget that all women share a spirituality of life, hope and endurance. May the lessons of our lives form a strong fabric of wisdom that binds us together, generation to generation.*

# The Brightest Stars

*"Look toward heaven and count the stars."*

Genesis 15:5

A distraught young mother called a friend, an older woman, and wept out her fatigue and frustration. She was at her wits end, feeling tied down and used up. The wise older woman later wrote the young mother the following letter:

> My heart goes out to you. I want you to remember that when you are feeling alone and exhausted, over half the world's population automatically extends comfort and spiritual support to you. I was often drained when my children were babies. I loved my children with the passion only a mother can know. But sometimes, late at night, I would sit outside on our cement step under the old elm, facing an open, summer night sky and wonder if I would ever again feel free, if I would ever again have the energy to enjoy dancing, if my children would ever be potty trained, if I would ever again feel like an individual.
>
> I know that right now you simply cannot comprehend the fact that you *will* know, once again, nights of refreshing, uninterrupted slumber. Your

children *will* learn not to eat dangerous things, not to dash out in front of cars, not to reach for hot things on the stove.

I remember many nights when my children and my husband were finally asleep. Although I was running on fumes and needed to be in bed myself, I just couldn't. Far more than sleep, I needed reflection time: time to think, to remember who I was. I needed time to dream my own dreams, hope my own hopes, and yes, cry the tears that erased the day's tension. What sweetness it was—to be alone facing the star-spangled sky and feeling the cool breeze against my silk night gown. I always felt my inner universe widen as I drank in that sacred solitude.

Believe it, young mother, when I tell you that you will barely remember the stress, the anxiety and the exhaustion. Sink into the discouragement you are feeling right now. Let the tears of frustration fall and drench your spirit with the relief of a good cry. Then, gather the strands of your scattered thoughts and think of ways that you can make small changes. Can you nap when the baby naps? Can some of your worries be put off until tomorrow? Can you take the phone off the hook for an hour? The greatest gift you can give yourself is to learn to live in the moment.

All of us who mother others in any way must focus on simplifying our lives as much as we can. We need to say no to outside demands and commitments, and we need to accept the fact that clutter and mess are simply part of the act of mothering. We need to remember that all of life is a sacrament of love—not only poured out for others but poured back with abundance into our own lives. It is in this exchange that ultimately we will find the secret to endurance.

*Enfolding Midwife God, promise that there will always be a bright, shining star of comfort on which to hang our blessings, prayers, hopes, dreams and tears.*

# Ka-Plop

*You have heard; now see all this;*
*and will you not declare it?*
*From this time forward, I make you hear*
*new things,*
*hidden things that you have not known.*
*They are created now; not long ago.*
Isaiah 48:6-7

Women often hear about the wisdom of "moving on" in life in order to behold its fullness. These words would be little more than inspirational platitudes, one woman writes, had she not experienced it herself.

I was walking in a park one afternoon and found navigating difficult due to a foot and a half of new-fallen snow. Ka-plop! I sank deep into the snow, up to my shins at every step. It took eight exhausting ka-plops just to get across a ditch. Even though I felt the invigorating surge of hot blood coursing through my sluggish, winter veins, I tired quickly and decided to turn around.

Standing there catching my breath, I looked at each deep footprint I had made, and I did not relish the hard work that my trip back would entail. And with that thought, I became aware of how my walk through the snow was similar to an ongoing personal issue I was wrestling with at the time. That struggle had caused me to feel iced in, as if my heart were encased by frost. In similar fashion, as I stood there in the snow that afternoon, it occurred to me that my feet were growing numb from the cold, that my teeth were beginning to chatter, and that my ears were burning. I realized how ridiculous it was to stay in one place if you are being frozen into immobility. I began stamping my feet to warm up, chuckling at the novelty of the analogy right before me.

As I decided to get moving on my return home, I also decided to "move on" in my life. As I put the first foot in the previously made footprint in the snow that afternoon, I was surprised to find that the ka-plopping was easy, *because I could step in the footprints I'd already made.*

In that moment, I knew that the concerns regarding my personal struggle were going to work out. I knew that the passion for life that had always carried me before would, in fact, carry me now. As I retraced my steps, ka-plop, ka-plop, it occurred to me that I had broken new ground not only in the new-fallen snow but inside myself as well. Sometimes we are called to break new ground in our attitudes in order to walk old ways.

We cannot always change the framework of our lives, but we need not sink in the freezing cold of helplessness as a result.

Rather, we can find new ways to live the familiar patterns of our lives with resilience, inner strength, humor, and even trusting in the power of small miracles. Thomas Merton had it right when he wrote, "Living is the constant adjustment of thought in such a way that we are always growing, always experiencing new things in the old and old things in the new. Thus, life is always new."

*God of All Millenniums, we celebrate because it is never too late to forge new tracks through old troubles. As new fallen snow, the future awaits our first hopeful footprint.*

# Imagine

*Nor to him who by the power at work
within us is able to accomplish abundantly
far more than all we can ask or imagine,
to him be glory, forever and ever.*

Ephesians 3:20–21

Imagine finding yourself more real than you've ever
been.

Imagine finding out you can take more than you think
you can.

Imagine finding great joy in simplicity, silence and
uncluttered thoughts.

Imagine the freedom found in the stripping away of
superficial masks.

Imagine the relief of a good day and not taking it for
granted.

Imagine finding soul mates who understand the
journey.

Imagine coping and deepening through pain and
hardship.

Imagine finding beauty in the most mundane,
ordinary things.

Imagine being at peace with mystery and the
unknown.

Imagine finding a partnership between inner strength and vulnerability.

Imagine believing God has a plan for your life.

Imagine taking pride in the ability to endure.

Imagine accepting imperfection in yourself and others.

Imagine being your own best friend.

Imagine being at home with the loss, confusion and revolution of faith that suffering entails.

Imagine adjusting and expanding in magnificent ways you never thought possible.

Imagine learning to live in the moment.

Imagine redefining yourself every day.

Imagine being human.

Imagine being heroic.

Imagine finding the light.

Imagine being light.

*God of Lanterns within Lanterns, we dwell always within the light of your love.*

# The Names of God

God of Lanterns within Our Breasts

God Who Mothers Starving Souls

God of Winding Roads and Unshakable Women

Great Physician of Tattered Horses and People in
Need of Mending

God of Broken Souls

Hovering, Ever-Present Mother God

God Who Loves Children, Animals and All That Is
Vulnerable

God Who Transcends Time and Space

God of Slumber

God of Heartaches in Progress

God of Empty Nests and Loved Ones Who Have
Crossed Over

God of Staircases to Heaven

Sweeping, Swooshing God Who Knows No
Boundaries

God Who Embraces Humankind

God of All That Goes Bump in the Night

God of People Hurt by the Failings of Others

Soul Mate God of Limitless Possibilities

God of Ships and Partners That Pass in the Night

Universe God Who Sets Us Early upon Your Knee

God of Young Mothers Who Grow Old

God Who Connects the Disconnected

God Who Knits Harmony into the Lives of All Sisters
God of Mothers and Daughters
Dream Builder God
God Who Frees Rivers and People
Soother of Wounds
God of Flowers That Bloom in the Night
God of Justice
God of Feminine Power and Authority
God of Wine and Roses
God Who Can Be All Things to All People
Multi-Faceted God Who Reveals Our Potential
God of Ancient Floods That Sweep the Human Heart
God of Holy Thursday and Good Friday
God of Solace
Go Who Overlaps Past, Present and Future
God of Women Still to Come
Enfolding Midwife God
God of All Millenniums
God of Lanterns within Lanterns

# Acknowledgments

I want to thank Julie Arvold, Julie Buntjer, Ardis Cloutier, OSF, Melanie Dunlap, Arlene Goetz, Judy Osgood, Frances Placentra, Mary Rademacher, Pat Samples, Melanie Schei, Karen Schuelke, Karen Warren Severson, Mary Southard, CSJ, Jamie Tuohy and Jennifer Wendler.

To the many who extended silent care, to those who shared their stories with me, and to Kass Dotterweich and Greg Pierce, my editor and publisher respectively, I extend my deepest gratitude.

# Additional Resources for Women

### Tall in Spirit
### Meditations for the Chronically Ill
Joni Woelfel

This best-seller is written in the same format as *The Light Within* and offers help to both people suffering from chronic illness and those who live or work with them. Written by a woman who suffers from several debilitating illnesses, this unique book offers spiritual and personal insights into coping with disease. (128-page paperback, $9.95)

### From Grief to Grace
### Images for Overcoming Sadness and Loss
Helen R. Lambin

A collection of images that assist people in naming, processing and overcoming grief caused by illness, a loved one's death, a job loss or similar difficult situations. (96-page paperback, $8.95)

### A Promise of Presence
### Weekly Reflections and Daily Prayer Activities
Bridget Mary Meehan and Regina M. Oliver

Fifty-two reflections on the belief that God's infinite presence permeates all of creation while seeking an intimate, personal relationship with each individual. Each reflection is followed by a seven-day prayer guide that provides clear directions for a week of creative, enriching prayer activities. (232-page paperback, $9.95)

### The Characters Within
### Befriending Your Deepest Emotions
Joy Clough, RSM

Explores the deepest human feelings, fears and motivations. Anguish, Blame, Delight, Exhilaration, Humility, Revenge, Vulnerability, Wonder and 50 other emotions come alive through these whimsical, anthropomorphic, evocative reflections. (160-page paperback, $9.95)

**Available from booksellers or call 800-397-2282 in the U.S. or Canada.**